MW00568881

# NASCAR SUPERSTARS

Escalator Press is an imprint of Stewart House Publishing Inc.
This edition is distributed by Stewart House Publishing Inc, Etobicoke, Canada.

This edition first published in 2002

10 9 8 7 6 5 4 3 2 1

A CIP catalogue reference for this book is available from the British Library.

ISBN 1 55366 280 6

Printed in Dubai


The author would like to thank Greg Fielden for his masterful *Forty Years Of
Stock Car Racing*, an invaluable source of information; R.J. Reynolds Tobacco
Company and Sports Marketing Enterprises for providing driver interview
opportunities and transcripts from the annual Winston Cup Preview; and
my wife, Lee Spencer, for her insight and support.


Project Editor: Luke Friend
Project Art Direction: Jim Lockwood
Production: Sarah Corteel
Picture Editor: Debora Fioravanti
Design: Brian Flynn

# NASCAR SUPERSTARS

Reid Spencer

ESCALATOR•press

# CONTENTS

# INTRODUCTION

**The face of stock car racing is changing, as NASCAR's elite division—the**

**Winston Cup Series—begins its high-speed journey through the 21st century.**

Long gone are the days when drivers clad in blue jeans and T-shirts manhandled cars with familiar names like Chevrolet, Oldsmobile, Ford, Mercury, Cadillac and Lincoln—along with such obsolete classics as Nash, Studebaker, Kaiser and the redoubtable Hudson Hornet—around Daytona's 4.15-mile Beach and Road Course.

Likewise relegated to the past are shoestring budgets and pit crews made up of family and friends. NASCAR today is high-tech and high-dollar. Corporate sponsors are willing to spend in excess of $15 million annually to have their logos painted on the hoods of the top drivers' cars.

No event on the Winston Cup schedule is more exciting than a night race at Bristol, one of the few traditional "short tracks" remaining on the circuit.

make from another, save for the nameplate and a few technical specifications not readily discernible to the eye—the height and width of the rear spoiler, or the length of the front air dam, for example.

Stock car racing has evolved from a regional sport indigenous to the southeast United States to a burgeoning national phenomenon. Thanks to an unprecedented growth of its fan base and a building boom during the last decade of the 20th century, "superspeedways" now dot the landscape in such diverse locales as Fort Worth, Texas; Kansas City, Missouri; Chicago, Illinois; Las Vegas, Nevada; and Fontana, California.

To the chagrin of traditionalists in the Bible Belt, these new monolithic rings of asphalt have begun to supplant the "short tracks" that were once the staple of stock car racing, but the influx of corporate dollars—not to mention a recent lucrative contract for the rights to televise the Winston Cup Series—demands a national presence and a corresponding foray into larger markets.

If the face of stock car racing is changing, so are the faces of its drivers. First and foremost, the composite Winston Cup driver of today is younger than his counterpart of a few years ago. The skill set, too, is radically different. No longer are daring and driving ability enough to carry the day. In a sport where the difference between winning and losing is measured in hundredths, or even thousandths, of a second, today's driver must be able to interpret changing track conditions and the subtle handling characteristics of his car and communicate them clearly to a crew chief whose function is to make critical, though often minute, adjustments throughout the course of a race.

Off the track, today's driver must also be a communicator—to potential consumers of his sponsor's product. The modern-era NASCAR superstar combines the highest level of performance with an ample dose of personal magnetism.

This book, then, is about the magnificent men who pilot the breathtaking machines of Winston Cup racing.

Those corporate dollars pay for wind tunnel testing; in-house engine shops that include the most sophisticated instrumentation available to the automotive industry; pit crews trained to change four tires and refuel a car in less than 15 seconds; and in the case of the most affluent teams, a support staff of 40 persons or more, ranging from the fabricators who construct the cars to the camp followers who handle the public relations machinery for their drivers.

No longer is there much that is "stock" about a stock car. Long gone are the days when drivers would tape up the headlights of their street cars and race them on a track, be it dirt or asphalt. The modern machines are sleek and aerodynamic, with engines capable of generating more than 750 horsepower. There is little to differentiate one

# The HISTORY

**Before Big Bill France's vision of a national sanctioning body became reality, stock car racing was a hit-or-miss proposition, to put it kindly.**

Rooted in the southeast region of the United States, the racing of stock cars can trace its origins—at least in part—to the manufacture and transport of illegal whiskey, otherwise known as "moonshine," throughout the backwoods of the south.

Outrunning government agents, known locally as "revenuers," required rather substantial modifications to existing street cars, especially where a full load of contraband was involved. Horsepower needed a significant boost, and stiffer springs were required to support the additional weight of the booze.

Racing the mechanically enhanced cars on short "bullrings" made of packed dirt evolved into a popular pastime. The growing sport, however, had no national governing body, no standardized set of rules, and no assurance that a track owner or promoter would be willing and able to pay the competitors at the end of the day.

Bill France sought to change all that and laid out his plan at a historic meeting at the Streamline Hotel in Daytona Beach on December 14, 1947. Two months later, the National Association for Stock Car Auto Racing was born, with France as its president.

Along with standardized rules, a points fund and a bona fide national championship came the iron-fisted rule of France. If NASCAR can be characterized as autocratic in its dealings with track owners and drivers—particularly in the early days—it is also necessary to understand that the sanctioning body was fighting for its life, and continued to do so in the face of challenges from rival organizations and the union movement.

The first race in NASCAR's "Strictly Stock" division, the entity that would eventually become the Winston Cup Series, took place on June 19, 1949 at Charlotte Speedway—not the 1.5-mile masterpiece that today dominates

**Bill France, the father of NASCAR.**

Highway 29 in Harrisburg, North Carolina, but a three-quarter-mile dirt oval on the outskirts of town.

The first Strictly Stock race produced the series' first disqualification. Glen Dunnaway was stripped of the victory when post-race inspection uncovered illegal springs on his 1947 Ford. Jim Roper of Kansas, who drove a 1949 Lincoln to second place on the track, inherited the win.

Five months later, the eight-race inaugural season of the Strictly Stock division concluded with Bob Flock's victory on the half-mile dirt track at North Wilkesboro, North Carolina. The series crowned its first champion, Robert "Red" Byron of Atlanta, Georgia, who accumulated 842.5 points to 725 for second-place Lee Petty.

### PETTY STARTS A DYNASTY

Ironically, both Byron and Petty felt the wrath of Bill France during the 1950 season, when NASCAR stripped them of championship points for competing in non-sanctioned events. Petty lost the first 809 points he earned during the season and finished third in the final standings behind Bill Rexford and Glenn "Fireball" Roberts.

Though he failed to win a series championship before his death in 1964 from injuries sustained in a fiery crash at Charlotte Motor Speedway, the gregarious Roberts emerged as stock car racing's first real superstar. But it was Petty who founded a dynasty that would dominate NASCAR racing for the better part of three decades.

Petty won his first championship in 1954 in a Chrysler and followed that with back-to-back titles in 1958 (in an Oldsmobile) and 1959 (in a Plymouth). It was also in 1959 that Lee and Richard Petty became the first father-son combination to finish first and second in the same NASCAR race, when they took the checkered flag at Atlanta. A year later they repeated the feat in Pittsburgh, Pennsylvania.

**Junior Johnson escapes through the rear window of his wrecked Pontiac at the Daytona Beach & Road Course in February 1956.**

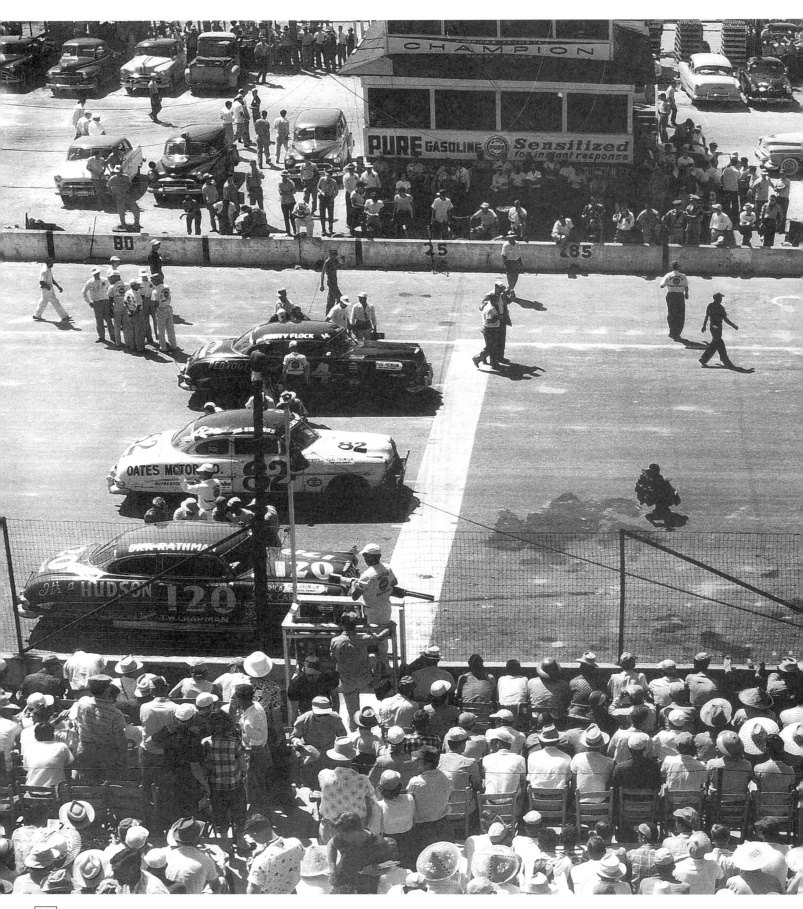

Richard Petty was a rookie during his father's championship season in 1958, but the man who would be "King" did not capture the first of his record 200 victories in NASCAR's elite series until 1960. Then the floodgates opened.

Petty won nine times and claimed the first of his seven series titles in 1964, but because of a Chrysler boycott resulting from France's decision to disallow the car maker's new hemi-head engine, Petty competed in just 14 races in 1965 and did not factor in the points race. Back in form in 1966, Petty won eight races and finished third in points behind David Pearson (who won 15 of the 42 events he entered) and James Hylton.

It was in 1967 that Petty left his indelible mark on the sport. With 27 victories and 38 top-fives in 48 races, the legend from Level Cross, North Carolina, won $150,000 and captured his second championship by more than 6,000 points over runner-up Hylton.

## THE CROWNING OF THE KING

Even more remarkable was the mind-boggling winning streak Petty fashioned that year. On August 12 he finished three laps ahead of Jim Paschal in the Myers Brothers Memorial race at Bowman Gray Stadium in Winston-Salem, North Carolina. It wasn't until October 15 at Charlotte that Petty would lose another race.

His string of ten straight wins lasted two months and included the storied Southern 500 at Darlington Raceway in South Carolina. No other driver has come close to equalling that mark. To racing fans, Petty's winning streak is just as "untouchable" as Joe DiMaggio's 56-game hitting streak is to baseball aficionados.

Though Petty would win five more titles before retiring after the 1992 season, his exploits in 1967 brought stock car racing squarely into the national spotlight. If Arnold Palmer propelled golf to the forefront in the 1960s, then Petty multiplied the popularity of stock car racing exponentially during the same decade. It is no accident that both Palmer and Petty are known in their respective sports simply as "The King."

The 1960s also saw the expansion of NASCAR's appeal in the consciousness of the auto racing community as a whole. The lure of intense competition drew such luminaries as Mario Andretti, Al Unser and A.J. Foyt—renowned for their open-wheeled exploits at Indianapolis—to the super-speedways of the South. Andretti won the Daytona 500 in 1967, Foyt in 1972. To this day, Andretti remains the only driver ever to have won the Indianapolis 500, the Daytona 500 and the Formula One driving world championship.

The main story of the 1960s, though, was Petty, and it is a source of no small degree of irony that the King did not receive the live television exposure he deserved during his peak years as a driver. Though R.J. Reynolds signed on as Winston Cup's title sponsor in 1971 and brought the vast marketing capabilities of that company into the equation, NASCAR's main event, the Daytona 500, was not televised live until 1979—Petty's final championship season.

Nonetheless, that inaugural broadcast was a watershed event for the sport. With one lap remaining, Cale Yarborough, Winston Cup champion in 1976, 1977 and 1978, and the only driver ever to win three straight titles, battled Donnie Allison for the lead.

Yarborough attempted to pass Allison on the back-stretch, but Allison's blocking maneuver forced Yarborough

**King Richard in all his glory.**

off the asphalt to the inside of the 2.5-mile superspeedway. As Yarborough returned to the racing surface, the cars collided, continued side-by-side, bumped several times and crashed in tandem into the third turn wall.

Mired in third place before the crash, Petty sped to a serendipitous victory, narrowly beating Darrell Waltrip to the finish line. But the CBS cameras focused on the fistfight that erupted between Yarborough and Bobby Allison, who stopped on the backstretch to check on the condition of his brother. Donnie soon joined the fray. That was mainstream America's introduction to big-time stock car racing.

## EMERGENCE OF EARNHARDT

In effect, the 1979 championship was Petty's swan-song. He won a total of ten races in the following five years, but the last victory—his 200th—again claimed the attention of the sporting world. On July 4, 1984, with the president of the United States, Ronald Reagan, in attendance, Petty won the Firecracker 400 at Daytona and added to a career victory total that is unlikely ever to be eclipsed.

If 1979 provided Petty with his final championship, it also served to introduce a brash young rookie from Kannapolis, North Carolina to followers of the sport. With an aggressive driving style, that in turn impressed and annoyed his fellow competitors, Dale Earnhardt won Winston Cup's Rookie of the Year crown that season. A year later, he would claim the first of his record-tying seven championships.

The 1980s brought the personalities of NASCAR into focus, from fast-talking Darrell Waltrip (nicknamed "Jaws" for his loquaciousness), to "Million Dollar" Bill Elliott, first winner of the Winston Million Bonus established by R.J. Reynolds. Add to the mix the irreverence of Tim Richmond (an enormously talented driver who contracted AIDS and died in 1989), the inexhaustible humor of Neil Bonnett (who died in a practice crash at Daytona in 1994), the self-assurance of Rusty Wallace, the dedication of Ricky Rudd, and the tenacity of Dave Marcis, a driver's driver who qualified for his final Daytona 500 in 2002, at age 60.

But until Jeff Gordon claimed his first championship in 1995, Earnhardt was the dominant driver in Winston Cup for more than ten years. And though Earnhardt won his final series title in 1994, he continued to dominate the sport with his unrelenting will to win. Despite Gordon's prodi-

**An empty grandstand presents a silent tribute to the late Dale Earnhardt.**

gious success, Earnhardt remained the primary focus of stock car racing until his death in the 2001 Daytona 500.

Earnhardt was a throwback to an earlier era. He was a master at getting the most from an ill-handling car. He was tight with a buck, thanks to a hard-scrabble upbringing that taught him the value of money. He inspired fanatic loyalty among his supporters and loathing among those who rooted against him. Because of Earnhardt's timely use of the "bump-and-run," the black No. 3 Chevy was the last thing another driver wanted to see in his rearview mirror.

And ironically, though Earnhardt steadfastly refused to wear a full-face crash helmet, his death has done more to promote safety enhancements in stock car racing than any other event in the history of the sport.

With Earnhardt departed, it is Gordon, more than any other driver, who has carried Winston Cup racing into the 21st century, and it is Gordon against whom pretenders to the throne will be measured.

The embodiment of the high-tech sophistication that now permeates the Winston Cup Series, Gordon has enjoyed a meteoric ascendance. Assisted by crew chief and mechanical guru Ray Evernham during his first three championship seasons (1995, 1997 and 1998), Gordon silenced skeptics in 2001 by winning the title with second-year crew chief Robbie Loomis (a veteran of Petty Enterprises) on the pit box.

Gordon is also at the vanguard of stock car racing's evolution toward multi-car teams. Gordon's car owner, Rick Hendrick, added a fourth team to his organization for 2002, to make room for rookie Jimmie Johnson. Car owner Jack Roush has employed as many as five Winston Cup drivers at the same time. Evernham, now heading the flagship organization for Dodge's return to Winston Cup, expanded his operation for 2002 with the addition of Jeremy Mayfield to a roster that already includes a pair of drivers at the opposite ends of the spectrum in terms of both age and experience—Casey Atwood, a rookie in 2001, and Elliott, a former champion.

It is against this backdrop that NASCAR's superstars of today will vie for supremacy.

# The DRIVERS

**What do NASCAR's superstars have in common? Without question, they all possess the ability to control a machine hurtling around a racetrack on the ragged edge between perfection and disaster. They revel in the mastery of man over that machine, even with the specter of serious injury or death as a constant companion, as they drive stock cars faster than they were ever meant to go.**

And to a man, they all enjoy the thrill of high-speed racing at close quarters, especially where an all-out dash to the checkered flag is concerned.

During the past decade, fans of Winston Cup racing have gotten to know a new generation of NASCAR superstars. Foremost among them is Jeff Gordon, a racing prodigy who began competing before he reached first grade. At age 30, Gordon already has four Winston Cup championships to his credit, and, in all likelihood, he will threaten the record seven titles shared by Richard Petty and Dale Earnhardt before his career is over.

Dale Earnhardt Jr. promises to carry on the tradition of his famous father, who died before his time in a last-lap crash at the 2001 Daytona 500. A driver in his father's image, Junior is an aggressive charger who has captivated the stock car racing audience with his fearless style.

If ever there was a driver who is "driven," it would have to be tempestuous Tony Stewart. A championship seems all but certain for the "Rushville Rocket," if he can remain focused on the job at hand. In 1999 Stewart accomplished what no other Winston Cup rookie had done before—he won three races.

There are other young guns to cheer for, even if they lack the pedigree of a Gordon, Earnhardt or Stewart. Twenty-one-year-old Casey Atwood showed enormous promise in his 2001 rookie season. Kevin Harvick won the third Winston Cup race he entered in 2001, at Atlanta, after taking over for the departed Dale Earnhardt.

**The most frenetic 15 seconds in major league sports—a pit stop under a caution flag.**

Driving for owner Jack Roush, Matt Kenseth edged Earnhardt Jr. for the Rookie of the Year title in 2000. Kurt Busch, another Roush protégé, had a solid inaugural season in 2001. Ryan Newman and Jimmie Johnson, a pair of rookies in 2002, may give the veterans a run for their money. Johnson won the pole for the 2002 Daytona 500 in his first attempt to qualify for the race.

Let's not forget the experienced 30- and 40-somethings who can still provide ample thrills for their supporters. Bill Elliott (the sport's perennial most popular driver), Rusty Wallace (the master of the short tracks), Dale Jarrett (with the mighty engines of Robert Yates powering his cars), Bobby Labonte (one of stock car racing's most consistent drivers), and brother Terry Labonte (a mainstay at Hendrick Motorsports) are all former series champions.

Two-time Daytona 500 winner Sterling Marlin saw his career rejuvenated in 2001 after Chip Ganassi bought the majority interest in Felix Sabates' SABCO racing teams and switched to Dodge. Ricky Rudd, who won at least one race per year from 1983 through 1998, battled Gordon for the 2001 title. Mark Martin and Jeff Burton represent Roush's best hopes to win a championship. Michael Waltrip broke a 462-race winless drought with his victory in the 2001 Daytona 500.

Ward Burton, Ricky Craven, Jerry Nadeau, Joe Nemechek, Jeremy Mayfield, Jimmy Spencer and Elliott Sadler all have Winston Cup victories to their credit, while Johnny Benson, Dave Blaney and Todd Bodine are all capable of posting a breakthrough win at any time.

Finding a NASCAR superstar to cheer for is not the problem. The difficulty lies in deciding which superstar to support.

# Casey ATWOOD

**If any driver embodies the youth movement in Winston Cup racing, that driver is Casey Atwood. The 21-year-old from Antioch, Tennessee, made his presence known on the national scene with a Busch Series victory at the Milwaukee Mile on July 4, 1999. At 18 years, ten months, nine days, Atwood became the youngest-ever winner of a Busch Series race.**

To those who had followed his career, that victory came as no surprise. Atwood had already won his first Busch Series pole at age 17 in his second start in the series in 1998. Trained in the late model stock car series at Highland Rim Speedway near Nashville, Atwood amassed more than a dozen victories before turning 16.

After qualifying fifth and finishing tenth at Homestead, Florida, in his third Winston Cup start in November 2000, Atwood completed his first full season in NASCAR's top series in 2001, driving a Dodge fielded by Ray Evernham. The team got off to a rocky start, but by season's end, Atwood was a contender. On October 28 he won his first Winston Cup pole at Phoenix International Raceway. A week later, at Rockingham, North Carolina, he qualified third.

On November 11 at Homestead, Atwood turned in a second-place qualifying performance and backed it up with his best Winston Cup Series finish of the year—third—as teammate Bill Elliott made a long-awaited visit to Victory Lane.

In the off-season, however, Atwood got word that he would no longer be driving Evernham's No. 19 Dodge. Instead, Atwood would move to the No. 7 Ultra Motorsports Dodge fielded by owner Jim Smith in partnership with Evernham for the 2002 season.

Atwood says he understands and accepts the change.

## STATS (SINCE 1997)

| YEAR | STARTS | WINS | TOP 5 | TOP 10 | MONEY |
|---|---|---|---|---|---|
| 2001 | 35 | 0 | 1 | 3 | $1,782,649 |
| 2000 | 3 | 0 | 0 | 1 | $97,030 |
| 1999 | did not compete | | | | |
| 1998 | did not compete | | | | |
| 1997 | did not compete | | | | |
| CAREER | 38 | 0 | 1 | 4 | $1,879,679 |

"I knew I was going to continue my relationship with Ray, and I knew we were starting up three teams and we were just going to expand the operation."

What has been much harder for Atwood to accept is the idea of not winning right away. Ever since he began his career in go-karts at age ten, Atwood has found his way to the winner's circle with relative ease. In the Winston Cup Series, he must keep his impatience in check.

"I won a lot of go-kart races when I first started," Atwood says. "I won a lot of late model races. It just keeps getting harder and harder every step you take. I won two Busch races my first season. This [Winston Cup] is by far the most competitive series I have ever been in … I think you could ever be in.

"It's hard to be patient. You've got to get the experience that you need to win. I think you can come in and win without experience if everything falls your way, but you can't come in and win consistently and run for a championship without experience, so you're just to going to have to wait it out and see what happens."

**7**

Birthdate: August 8, 1980

Birthplace: Antioch, TN

Team: Ultra Motorsports

Sponsor: Sirius Satellite Radio

Owners: Jim Smith, Ray Evernham

Crew Chief: Tony Furr

Car: Dodge

**With Ray Evernham's support, Casey Atwood has high expectations.**

# Johnny **BENSON**

**Ever since his Rookie of the Year season in 1996, Johnny Benson has been threatening to win a Winston Cup race, but Murphy's Law seems to rule Benson's life when it comes to closing the deal.**

A driver of undeniable talent and a former champion in NASCAR's Busch Series as well as the American Speed Association (ASA) Series, Benson won the pole at Atlanta in his fourth Winston Cup start in 1996. That same year, driving for owner Chuck Rider, he posted six top-ten finishes, including an eighth in the vaunted Brickyard 400 at Indianapolis, where he led the race only to fade in the closing laps.

After an 11th-place points finish in 1997, Benson moved to Roush Racing in 1998 and scored three top-five finishes, but the promise he showed that year failed to carry over into 1999. Benson obtained his release from Roush at the end of the season and signed on with Tyler Jet Motorsports for 2000. He led the Daytona 500 with four laps remaining, but crossed the finish line in 12th as the lead pack reshuffled in the closing moments of the race.

At mid-season, Benson's team changed hands, and he became a de facto team-mate of Ken Schrader at MB2 Motorsports. Neverthelesss, Benson posted a career-best second-place finish for each of his owners in 2000, improving from a 33rd-place start to the runner-up position at the Spring race at Bristol and parlaying a third-place qualifying effort into a second-place result at Dover Downs in September.

In 2001, Benson again finished 11th in the Winston Cup standings. After the Daytona 500, he ran off a fine string of four straight top-tens, including a fourth at Darlington.

Benson subsequently posted three third-place finishes, at Texas in April, at the Brickyard in August, and at

| STATS (SINCE 1997) | | | | | |
|---|---|---|---|---|---|
| **YEAR** | **STARTS** | **WINS** | **TOP 5** | **TOP 10** | **MONEY** |
| 2001 | 36 | 0 | 6 | 14 | $2,894,903 |
| 2000 | 33 | 0 | 3 | 7 | $1,841,324 |
| 1999 | 34 | 0 | 0 | 2 | $1,567,668 |
| 1998 | 32 | 0 | 3 | 10 | $1,360,335 |
| 1997 | 32 | 0 | 0 | 8 | $1,256,457 |
| **CAREER** | **197** | **0** | **13** | **47** | **$9,867,767** |

Rockingham in November. But in a season where first-time winners seemed almost commonplace, victory continued to elude the Michigan native.

Despite coming up empty in 197 consecutive Winston Cup starts entering the 2002 season, Benson seems content to let things take their natural course.

"I think it's great that we've had a lot of first-time winners," Benson says. "We're disappointed we weren't one of them. By the same token, we've been competitive week-in, week-out and running up front. I think that's more important to me, to make sure we run consistently and run consistently good week-in, week-out than to worry about having to win a race and then be 30th in points. I don't want that, either.

"So I think we'll get our wins, and they'll come when it happens. We'll win our race and we'll get where we need— hopefully in the top five in points, because that's the goal to get to."

Unfortunately for Benson, the 2002 season did not begin auspiciously. After a 10th-place finish in the season-opening Daytona 500, Benson twice slipped as low as 30th in points before recovering to 27th with a 15th-place result at Fontana, California.

**Johnny Benson has the talent to win, but bad luck seems to strike at the most unexpected moments.**

10

Birthdate: June 27, 1963
Birthplace: Grand Rapids, MI
Team: MBV Motorsports
Sponsor: Valvoline
Owner: Nelson Bowers
Crew Chief: James Ince
Car: Pontiac

# Dave BLANEY

**If nothing else, Dave Blaney has learned to adapt to change.**

Like former Sprint Car champion Steve Kinser before him, Blaney has struggled to find a consistent level of performance in the stock car ranks. On the other hand, he has displayed, on more than a few occasions, the depth of his driving talent.

Blaney won the 1995 World of Outlaws championship and was named Sprint Car Driver of the Year that same season. In 1999, he finished seventh in the Busch Series standings despite missing one event due to a scheduling conflict with one of his five starts in the Winston Cup. He won four Busch Series poles, posted 13 top-tens and twice finished second in 1999, at Atlanta in March and at Darlington in September. In his five Winston Cup events with Bill Davis Racing, he qualified fourth and finished 23rd at Homestead for his best results in each category.

Blaney's rookie season in the Winston Cup (2000) was an up-and-down affair. Though he claimed a pair of top-ten finishes, he failed to complete seven races. Davis switched his teams from Pontiac to Dodge for 2001, and despite the complications inherent in a change-over from one make to another, Blaney can point to one formidable accomplishment during his sophomore season—he qualified for all 36 Winston Cup events. Three times he finished sixth—at Texas in April, in the Pepsi 400 at Daytona in July and at Rockingham in October—for his best results of the campaign. The 2001 season also brought a career-best finish in the points standings—22nd, one notch ahead of two-time series champion Terry Labonte—and a career-best year for prize money, more than $1.8 million.

But 2002 brought more change for Blaney. He left Davis and signed on with the Jasper Engines, replacing Robert Pressley in the No. 77 car. That move also meant a switch to Ford and the chance to work with crew chief Ryan Pemberton.

"I'm going to try them all out before I find one I like," was Blaney's tongue-in-cheek comment about the frequent changes in manufacturers. "We're set for two years with Jasper and Ford has got a great track record. They have got some awful good race teams. We're hooked up a little bit with the Penske group with the engines, and hope we can work with Rusty [Wallace] and Ryan [Newman] and make us all three better."

Blaney competed in his first Winston Cup race in a Pontiac, but not in one owned by Bill Davis. Before 1999, his only Cup experience came at Rockingham in 1992, where he completed 371 of 492 laps in the Steve Hover Pontiac and finished 31st.

Blaney hasn't abandoned his involvement with Sprint Cars. He owns the World of Outlaws team for which his brother, Dale Blaney, drives.

## STATS (SINCE 1997)

| YEAR | STARTS | WINS | TOP 5 | TOP 10 | MONEY |
|------|--------|------|-------|--------|-------|
| 2001 | 36 | 0 | 0 | 6 | $1,827,296 |
| 2000 | 33 | 0 | 0 | 2 | $1,272,689 |
| 1999 | 5 | 0 | 0 | 0 | $212,170 |
| 1998 | did not compete | | | | |
| 1997 | did not compete | | | | |
| CAREER | 75 | 0 | 0 | 8 | $3,317,255 |

**Easy-going and pensive off the track, Dave Blaney is a charger behind the wheel.**

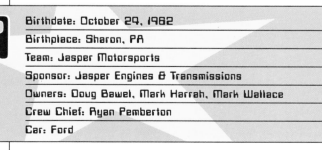

**77**

Birthdate: October 24, 1982
Birthplace: Sharon, PA
Team: Jasper Motorsports
Sponsor: Jasper Engines & Transmissions
Owners: Doug Bawel, Mark Harrah, Mark Wallace
Crew Chief: Ryan Pemberton
Car: Ford

# Todd BODINE

**Perhaps the number "13" will be lucky for Todd Bodine. After all, he married his wife Lynn on Friday, November 13, 1987.**

Thirteen is also the number of different Winston Cup car owners Bodine has driven for in the past 11 years, dating to his single-race debut for Junie Donlavey in 1992.

Since then, Bodine can count among his employers—often in a fill-in capacity—Butch Mock, Bill Elliott, David Blair, Andy Petree, Rick Hendrick, brother Geoff Bodine, Frank Cicci, Buz McCall, Bob Hancher, Joe Falk, Jack Birmingham, and Travis Carter.

It was with Carter in 2001 that Bodine competed in his first full season of Winston Cup since running 28 races for Mock in 1995. Despite 145 starts in NASCAR's top series, Bodine has yet to win a race. Then again, the youngest of three racing brothers from Chemung, New York, has seldom been around long enough to fulfill his potential as a driver.

The 2001 season was one of mixed results for Bodine. His qualifying effort was spectacular, with five front-row starts that included poles at Chicago, Pocono and Martinsville. His results, however, were less than inspiring. He finished fifth at Las Vegas in March and matched that season-best effort at Watkins Glen in August. Those were Bodine's only top-tens for the entire year. Those two results, however, did increase his total of career top-fives from four to six.

Though team-mate Jimmy Spencer departed at the end of the season for the Chip Ganassi organization, to be replaced by Joe Nemechek, Bodine was hoping to build on the positive aspects of the 2001 season in 2002, but the bankruptcy of his primary sponsor, Kmart, left

| STATS (SINCE 1997) | | | | | |
|---|---|---|---|---|---|
| **YEAR** | **STARTS** | **WINS** | **TOP 5** | **TOP 10** | **MONEY** |
| 2001 | 35 | 0 | 2 | 2 | $1,740,315 |
| 2000 | 5 | 0 | 0 | 1 | $234,065 |
| 1999 | 7 | 0 | 0 | 0 | $208,382 |
| 1998 | 14 | 0 | 1 | 2 | $378,766 |
| 1997 | 5 | 0 | 0 | 0 | $125,845 |
| **CAREER** | **145** | **0** | **6** | **16** | **$4,111,564** |

Bodine and the entire Carter organization facing an uncertain future as they prepared to compete in the 2002 Daytona 500.

With money in the bank for the first two races of the season, however, Bodine was more concerned with the performance of his car as Speedweeks approached. Improving on the 39th-place start and 34th-place finish from a year earlier was foremost on his mind.

"I think that our team has a little work to do," Bodine said. "We've got a good direction to negotiate. We know some things that are going to pick the car up and, naturally, we're driving a Ford and we need some help there. (Sure enough, the Fords subsequently got a rules concession from NASCAR.)

"I think we're going to get up yet. Hopefully, we'll go back and be competitive. We are definitely better than we were last year, which is a big plus."

Bodine already has 11 Busch Series victories to his credit. With a little good luck, for a change, he may well add his name to the list of Winston Cup winners before long.

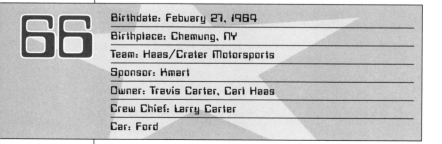

**66**

Birthdate: Febuary 27, 1964
Birthplace: Chemung, NY
Team: Haas/Crater Motorsports
Sponsor: Kmart
Owner: Travis Carter, Carl Haas
Crew Chief: Larry Carter
Car: Ford

**Todd Bodine has driven for 13 different Winston Cup owners in 11 seasons.**

# Jeff BURTON

**Most drivers would have taken Jeff Burton's 2001 season and walked away well satisfied. After all, the Virginia driver won two races—the prestigious Coca-Cola 600 at Lowe's Motor Speedway in Charlotte and the Checker Auto Parts/Dura-Lube 500 at Phoenix. In the process, the younger of the two Burton brothers won more than $3.7 million.**

But for Burton, 2001 was a step backwards; a change of direction in a career that had been an unrelenting ascent to the top level of his sport. Burton was tenth in the Winston Cup standings, but that was the first time since 1996 that he had finished outside the top five. The 2001 season also broke a streak of success where each year was better than its predecessor.

Driving for the Stavola Brothers team, Burton won the Winston Cup Rookie of the Year crown in 1994. After again spending the 1995 season with the Stavolas team, Burton jumped at the chance to drive for Jack Roush in 1996 and has been with Roush ever since.

Burton won his first Winston Cup race at Texas in April 1997, and before the season was over, he had collected his second and third victories—at New Hampshire and Martinsville. He was the model of consistency with 13 top-five finishes and 18 top-tens. His first foray into the elite top ten in the points standings was also his first visit to the rarified air of the top five—Burton was fourth at the end of the year.

The 1998 season brought two more wins, 18 top-fives, 23 top-tens and a fifth-place points finish, but that was just a harbinger of what was to come in 1999.

## STATS (SINCE 1997)

| YEAR | STARTS | WINS | TOP 5 | TOP 10 | MONEY |
|---|---|---|---|---|---|
| 2001 | 36 | 2 | 8 | 16 | $4,230,737 |
| 2000 | 34 | 4 | 15 | 22 | $5,959,439 |
| 1999 | 34 | 6 | 18 | 23 | $5,725,399 |
| 1998 | 33 | 2 | 18 | 23 | $2,626,987 |
| 1997 | 32 | 3 | 13 | 18 | $2,296,614 |
| CAREER | 259 | 17 | 81 | 119 | $22,958,499 |

With six victories—at Charlotte, New Hampshire, Las Vegas, Rockingham, and both Darlington races (including the coveted Southern 500)—Burton earned a career-best $5,725,399 and another fifth in the season standings.

With 2000 came Burton's highest finish in the points—third—and four more victories. In one of those wins, New Hampshire, he accomplished the rare feat of leading all 300 laps.

Not surprisingly, Burton was considered a formidable contender for the Winston Cup championship in 2001. Surprisingly, he wasn't a threat. Never a strong qualifier, Burton had always been able to count on his ability to work his way to the front during the course of a race. In 2001, his Fords lacked their customary muscle.

"Even though we did put a string of good races together toward the end of the year … we didn't lead enough laps, which means we weren't as fast as we needed to be," Burton said of the disappointing season.

"If we're going to win the championship or even contend for the championship, we've got to be consistent—and you can't be consistent and be slow … If

Birthdate: June 29, 1967
Birthplace: South Boston, VA
Team: Roush Racing
Sponsor: CITGO Racing
Owner: Jack Roush
Crew Chief: Frank Stoddard
Car: Ford

we're going to win the championship, we've got to go faster."

But don't write Burton off yet. Don't let one "off" year cloud your judgment. He has a solid team and an excellent relationship with crew chief Frank Stoddard. His 17 wins on the circuit place him in elite company. Chances are, he'll be at the top of the standings soon enough.

Above: Jeff Burton (No. 99) goes three-wide with Mark Martin (No. 6) and John Andretti (No. 43). Left: Burton celebrates in Victory Lane at Phoenix.

# Ward **BURTON**

**Everybody in the NASCAR garage does an impression of Ward Burton, because his unmistakable slow Virginia drawl is so much fun to mimic.**

Burton's laid-back personality matches his speech pattern, until he climbs behind the wheel. That is where his competitive fire manifests itself, the same sort of drive that earned him top ranking on Hargrave Military Academy's rifle team during his high school days in Virginia.

On the track, Burton is a charger, as he has demonstrated consistently during his Winston Cup career. In his first season, racing for A.G. Dillard in 1994, Burton won the pole for the October race in Charlotte. After moving to Bill Davis Racing for the final nine races of the 1995 season, Burton posted his first Winston Cup victory in the fall race at Rockingham.

His next victory would not come until the March 2000 race at Darlington, though Burton did accumulate three second-place finishes in 1999. In fact, Burton found himself in the championship mix early in 2000 with eight top-tens in the first 13 races. At that time he was second in the Winston Cup points standings, but the balance of the season wasn't as kind to the No. 22 Caterpillar team. By season's end Burton had fallen to tenth in the standings. And 2000 also marked the first time in five years that Burton failed to win a pole.

With Davis Racing's switch from Pontiac to Dodge in 2001 came the most significant victory of Burton's career—a win at the Southern 500 in Darlington. That race, however, was the high watermark in an otherwise inconsistent year that saw Burton fall to 14th in Winston Cup points.

But the driver who jokingly refers to himself as "Ranger Rick" because of his very serious involvement in wildlife

| STATS (SINCE 1997) | | | | | |
|---|---|---|---|---|---|
| **YEAR** | **STARTS** | **WINS** | **TOP 5** | **TOP 10** | **MONEY** |
| 2001 | 34 | 1 | 6 | 10 | $3,583,692 |
| 2000 | 34 | 1 | 4 | 17 | $2,699,604 |
| 1999 | 34 | 0 | 6 | 16 | $2,405,913 |
| 1998 | 33 | 0 | 1 | 5 | $1,516,183 |
| 1997 | 31 | 0 | 0 | 7 | $1,004,944 |
| **CAREER** | **250** | **3** | **21** | **67** | **$13,023,310** |

preservation and conservation looks to a more stable future. The driver who operates the Ward Burton Wildlife Foundation is also interested in preserving the status quo at Bill Davis Racing, and in 2002, he got his wish.

"This is really the first year at Bill Davis Racing that we haven't gone through a huge change," Burton said, as he prepared to qualify for the 2002 Daytona 500. "Last year it was going to Dodge. The year before that it was starting a new Winston Cup team. Now, Tommy Baldwin (Burton's crew chief) has had time to get everything in place where he thought it needed to be."

Will continuity lead to a championship for Burton, either in 2002 or farther down the road? Stranger things have happened in stock car racing. And Burton's victory in the 2002 Daytona 500 wasn't a bad way to start the rest of his career.

## 22

Birthdate: October 25, 1961
Birthplace: South Boston, VA
Team: Bill Davis Racing
Sponsor: Caterpillar
Owner: Bill Davis
Crew Chief: Tommy Baldwin Jr.
Car: Dodge

**A conservationist at heart, Ward Burton is anything but conservative on the racetrack.**

# Kurt BUSCH

**The unqualified success of such young drivers as Jeff Gordon and Tony Stewart increases the pressure on other owners to sign the next "young gun" to a Winston Cup contract. That temptation can sometimes lead to the premature promotion of an inexperienced driver to NASCAR's highest level.**

When Jack Roush announced in 2000 that he was adding Kurt Busch to his roster of Winston Cup drivers, there were skeptics. After all, Busch had come to the owner's attention during a series of try-outs known as the "Gong Shows." Prior to signing on with Roush as a trainee in NASCAR's Craftsman Truck Series, Busch had limited, albeit successful, racing experience—in Legends Cars, Dwarf Cars and NASCAR's Featherlite Southwest Tour, where he won the series championship in 1999.

Busch soon made believers of his doubters, and his deep reservoir of driving talent proved more than enough to offset his sketchy resume. He won four Truck Series races in 2000 to go with a pair of top-ten qualifying efforts in the seven Winston Cup races he entered as preparation for a full schedule in 2001.

Sure, there were growing pains in his first full season of Cup racing, but Busch showed flashes of brilliance. He posted his first top-five finish in the seventh race of the season, at Texas, where he crossed the finish line in fourth place. Two races later, he finished third at the world's fastest closed course, the 2.66-mile tri-oval at Talladega. A fifth place at the Brickyard 400 in August proved Busch could also negotiate a flat track.

Predictably inconsistent during his freshman season, Busch was 27th in the points, but he finished ahead of a number of series regulars, among them Todd Bodine, Joe Nemechek and John Andretti.

Busch entered the 2002 season with an optimistic outlook, buoyed by his taste of success in 2001. Perhaps his approach to the qualifying races at Daytona also sums up his attitude as a driver.

"I love the pressure," Busch says. "It's what I live off. I love to be the guy that the pressure is on, to have it on my shoulders so I can pull through and do it for the team."

Busch's younger brother Kyle is also a talented young driver, but NASCAR recently put a stop to his career in the Craftsman Truck series by imposing a new rule requiring drivers to be 18 years old. Kyle was 16 at the time.

"He should have been grandfathered in on that age rule," Kurt Busch said. "That would have been the right decision, I believe."

Then again, Busch isn't exactly mainstream when it comes to the NASCAR community. He prefers alternative rock music (Metallica in particular) to country and western, the stock car racing staple. He's also an avid Chicago Cubs fan.

Let's hope Busch doesn't find a championship as elusive as the Cubs have.

**With a deep reservoir of talent, Kurt Busch is well on his way to stardom on the Winston Cup circuit.**

## STATS (SINCE 1997)

| YEAR | STARTS | WINS | TOP 5 | TOP 10 | MONEY |
|------|--------|------|-------|--------|-------|
| 2001 | 35 | 0 | 3 | 6 | $2,170,629 |
| 2000 | 7 | 0 | 0 | 0 | $311,915 |
| 1999 | did not compete | | | | |
| 1998 | did not compete | | | | |
| 1997 | did not compete | | | | |
| TOTAL | 42 | 0 | 3 | 6 | $2,482,544 |

**97**

Birthdate: August 9, 1978
Birthplace: Las Vegas, NV
Team: Roush Racing
Sponsor: Rubbermaid
Owner: Jack Roush
Crew Chief: Jimmy Fennig
Car: Ford

# Ricky CRAVEN

**The 2001 season was a vindication for Ricky Craven. The obituary for Craven's career had been written three years earlier, when post-concussion syndrome forced him to resign from Hendrick Motorsports during the 1998 season. But he proved his doubters wrong.**

His tenure with Hendrick had begun with such promise. After two full seasons driving for car owner Larry Hedrick—a stint that included two of the most spectacular crashes ever caught on videotape, in 1996 at Talladega and Charlotte—Craven jumped ship to Hendrick for the 1997 season.

The three Hendrick team-mates—Jeff Gordon, Terry Labonte and Craven—finished one-two-three in the season-opening Daytona 500, and expectations for Craven became enormous. But a practice accident at Texas forced the driver from Newburgh, Maine, to sit out two races, and the after-effects of that accident would have a profound influence on both his life and his career for years to come.

Four races into the 1998 season, Craven could not drive anymore. He missed 13 races battling post-concussion syndrome. It was at New Hampshire that Craven decided to make his return. Miraculously, he won the pole, but he faded to a disappointing 29th in the race itself. Three races later, after a 35th-place finish at Watkins Glen, Craven left Hendrick.

In 1999 and 2000, Craven ran a limited scheduled, driving for first for Scott Barbour and then for Hal Hicks. His performances were impressive enough to attract the attention of owner Cal Wells III, who signed Craven for 2001 with Tide as the primary sponsor.

Craven made the most of the opportunity. In a season that featured three top-five finishes, Craven notched his first Winston Cup victory in 174 starts on October 14 at Martinsville, where he won in a shoot-out with 1999 series champion Dale Jarrett.

"It took a long time," Craven said. "It [the list of Winston Cup winners] is still an elite group, an exclusive group, when you consider how short the list is. And then when you look at it in terms of the modern era, there is a small group and I admire everyone that's done it.

"After you win, expectations change forever. Once you clear that hurdle, then the expectations are you should be able to do this more often—and it is just not easy. It took me 174 races, and I won't wait that long for the second one. Hopefully, it'll come sooner."

One by-product of Craven's own difficulties is his firm commitment to charity. He works with the Children's Miracle Network, the National Bone Marrow Foundation (car owner Rick Hendrick is a leukemia survivor), Make-A-Wish Foundation and Travis Roy Foundation. Every year Craven holds a fund-raising snowmobile ride in Maine.

## STATS (SINCE 1997)

| YEAR | STARTS | WINS | TOP 5 | TOP 10 | MONEY |
|---|---|---|---|---|---|
| 2001 | 36 | 1 | 4 | 7 | $1,996,981 |
| 2000 | 16 | 0 | 0 | 0 | $636,562 |
| 1999 | 24 | 0 | 0 | 0 | $853,835 |
| 1998 | 11 | 0 | 0 | 1 | $527,875 |
| 1997 | 30 | 0 | 4 | 7 | $1,259,550 |
| CAREER | 180 | 1 | 11 | 24 | $6,817,566 |

## 32

Birthdate: May 24, 1966
Birthplace: Bangor, ME
Team: PPI Motorsports
Sponsor: Tide
Owner: Cal Wells III
Crew Chief: Mike Beam
Car: Ford

**Ricky Craven celebrates his long-awaited first Winston Cup victory at Martinsville in 2001.**

# Dale EARNHARDT JR.

**If there is one indelible snapshot of Dale Earnhardt Jr.'s young life, it is the emotional celebration at Daytona in July of 2001—the third-generation driver standing in jubilation atop his No. 8 Chevrolet, hugged by DEI teammate and friend Michael Waltrip.**

Earnhardt had just sped to a dominating victory in the Pepsi 400, in effect conquering the speedway that had taken the life of his legendary father just five months earlier. For Junior, the victory was more than redemption. It was an indication to the world that he had learned to live with the pain of his loss and had translated that pain into performance.

It was Earnhardt's third Winston Cup victory, and to that point, the defining moment in his short career.

"I had hard core emotions about going back after my father's death," Earnhardt says.

"Everybody knows the story. Had fun there and went to the race with a strong will; won the race and … with all that happened, I have made my peace with that place or straightened out any wrinkles we might have had in our relationship, so I look forward to going back—because I love Daytona. I always have, always will; going into that place, I probably won't have the same emotion as most people. Most people might be depressed or upset, but I'm going to keep on being upbeat and having a damn good time."

The Pepsi 400 was also a break-out victory for Earnhardt, who won twice more before the end of the season—at Dover and at Talladega. He finished eighth in the points standings.

Earnhardt embarked on his professional driving career at age 17. What other career path was the son of a seven-time Winston Cup champion going to follow? In the early days, he raced against his brother Kerry and sister Kelley in late model stock cars.

His rise through the ranks of NASCAR's touring series was meteoric. In 1997, he entered eight Busch Series events. In 1998, he won the championship in that division. Earnhardt won six races and added another Busch Series title to his portfolio in 1999. By 2000, he was ready for a full-time ride in the Winston Cup Series, in a car owned by his father.

Earnhardt's rookie season brought two victories, the first coming at Texas, the second at Richmond. More importantly, he proved he could perform at peak levels, despite the onerous expectations that came with being his father's son. Ironically, Earnhardt did not win Winston Cup's Rookie of the Year crown, a feat accomplished by his father in 1979. Instead, the title went to Matt Kenseth, one of Roush Racing's young stars and a protégé of veteran Mark Martin.

Then came Daytona 2001, where Earnhardt chased Waltrip to the finish line while his father sat lifeless in his crumpled black No. 3 Chevy a few hundred yards behind. But as he says, Earnhardt Jr. has made his peace with Daytona. Now he looks ahead toward the championship he needs to establish his own legend.

"There's more to me, I think, professionally than just magazine covers and kick-ass sponsors and fun times," Earnhardt says, referring to his appearances in *Rolling Stone* and *People*, the latter of which included him on a list of "Sexiest Men." "I want to win championships and I like winning races. We celebrate ours and enjoy that. We look

Birthdate: October 10, 1979
Birthplace: Kannapolis, NC
Team: Dale Earnhardt Incorporated
Sponsor: Budweiser
Owner: Teresa Earnhardt
Crew Chief: Tony Eury Sr.
Car: Chevrolet

**Third-generation driver Dale Earnhardt Jr. seems well-equipped to carry the torch passed on by his legendary father.**

forward to winning more, but there's a side from just winning the championship and all the celebration and the extras and whatnot that come along with that.

"There's something to be said about having that asterisk beside your name for the rest of your life and the rest of the time in the books that says you were champion sometime in your life. So that's something I'd like to be a part of. I can see that I really have a great opportunity to take it to several levels and to be somebody that is maybe in the same sentence with several of the greats in the sport down

> # "There's more to me, I think, than just magazine covers and kick-ass sponsors and fun times. "

the road—so I need to win some championships."

Earnhardt drives the No. 8 car to honor his grandfather, Ralph Earnhardt, a North Carolina short-track star who used the same number. For a certainty, Dale Jr. has inherited the talents of his predecessors in the family, including the aggressive driving style.

**The No. 8 Budweiser Chevrolet has become a dominant force at NASCAR's two restrictor-plate racetracks, Daytona and Talladega.**

## STATS (SINCE 1997)

| YEAR | STARTS | WINS | TOP 5 | TOP 10 | MONEY |
|------|--------|------|-------|--------|-------|
| 2001 | 36 | 3 | 9 | 15 | $5,827,542 |
| 2000 | 34 | 2 | 3 | 5 | $2,801,880 |
| 1999 | 5 | 0 | 0 | 1 | $162,095 |
| 1998 | did not compete | | | | |
| 1997 | did not compete | | | | |
| **CAREER** | **75** | **5** | **12** | **21** | **$8,791,517** |

# Bill ELLIOTT

**After the success of the Petty empire began to wane in the early to mid-1980s, Bill Elliott proved that a family operation could still get the job done.**

The 46-year-old Georgia driver made his first start in Winston Cup more than a quarter of a century ago. The driver who would become "Million Dollar Bill" won $640 in that first race at Rockingham in 1976. After six years without a victory, Elliott signed on with Harry Melling, who added his considerable financial muscle to the team. Brother Ernie Elliott continued to provide the mechanical genius and the horsepower.

A year later, "Awesome Bill from Dawsonville" won his first race in his 117th start at Riverside (Cal.) International Raceway, a road course. His third-place finish in the 1983 points standings promised better things to come. In 1984, Elliott won three races and again finished third, but 1985 brought one of the most spectacular seasons in the history of Winston Cup racing.

Elliott visited Victory Lane 11 times, finished second in the points and became the first driver to claim the Winston Million Bonus offered by R.J. Reynolds Tobacco Company for any driver who could win three of four designated races. Elliott claimed the prize with victories in the Daytona 500, the Winston 500 at Talladega and the Southern 500 at Darlington.

In 1986, he won twice, both times at Michigan, captured the Winston All-Star event at Charlotte (a race that does not count in the championship standings) and qualified on pole four times. After that "mediocre" season, Elliott began his climb to the top of the mountain. In 1987, he won six times and finished second in points. A year later, he won his only series championship, again with six victories. But after winning only five more races over the next three years, Elliott left

## STATS (SINCE 1997)

| YEAR | STARTS | WINS | TOP 5 | TOP 10 | MONEY |
|------|--------|------|-------|--------|-------|
| 2001 | 36 | 1 | 5 | 9 | $3,618,017 |
| 2000 | 32 | 0 | 3 | 7 | $2,580,823 |
| 1999 | 34 | 0 | 1 | 2 | $1,624,101 |
| 1998 | 32 | 0 | 0 | 5 | $1,618,421 |
| 1997 | 32 | 0 | 5 | 14 | $1,607,827 |
| **CAREER** | **659** | **41** | **160** | **294** | **$27,306,174** |

Melling in 1992 to drive for legendary owner Junior Johnson, who had won 50 races during his own career as a driver.

Elliott's inaugural season with Johnson produced five victories and a second-place finish in the series standings, but in his last two seasons with the former "moonshiner" from North Wilkesboro, North Carolina, Elliott won only once more—in the 1994 Southern 500.

Returning to the track as an owner/driver in 1995, Elliott endured six years of frustration. His best finish during that span was second at the first Michigan race of 1997. When Ray Evernham offered Elliott the opportunity to lead Dodge's return to Winston Cup racing, Elliott was ready.

He won the pole for the season-opening Daytona 500 in 2001 and ended his victory drought with a win from pole at Homestead in November.

"Last year took a lot of pressure off us, Ray, the whole deal," Elliott said of the 2001 season. "If you put things into perspective, once I left Junior in 1994, put my deal together in 1995 and then tried to make the deal work—and we worked so hard to make the deal work—we could never accomplish the goals that we set out to do. It was always a constant battle year-in, year-out. I'll always remember every winter when the last race was over you fought the same battles coming back to Daytona."

Backed by Evernham and Dodge, Elliott hopes the struggles are over as he continues to build on his recent success.

**9**

Birthdate: October 8, 1955
Birthplace: Cumming, GA
Team: Evernham Motorsports
Sponsor: Dodge Dealers/UAW
Owner: Ray Evernham
Crew Chief: Mike Ford
Car: Dodge

**"Awesome Bill from Dawsonville" won from the pole at Homestead, Florida in 2001.**

# Jeff GORDON

**It is difficult to believe that a driver who won three Winston Cup championships and claimed more than 50 victories before his 29th birthday would still have much to prove—but that was the case with Jeff Gordon.**

Despite the phenomenal success he had enjoyed before the 2000 season, NASCAR's Wunderkind had his doubters. There were those who believed that most of the credit for Gordon's formidable results belonged to the Hendrick Motorsports organization (with its seemingly limitless resources) and the know-how of crew chief Ray Evernham, who made the calls from the pits in each of Gordon's championship runs in 1995, 1997 and 1998.

The nay-sayers were convinced that Evernham's departure at the end of the 1999 season, to spearhead the return of Dodge to Winston Cup racing, would diminish the magnitude of Gordon's stardom. In 2000, it appeared the doubters might be right. Gordon struggled as he and new crew chief Robbie Loomis began the acclimation process. Gordon also had a new "over-the-wall gang" to deal with in the pits, after the defection of the nucleus of the vaunted "Rainbow Warriors" to Robert Yates Racing.

Nevertheless, Gordon managed three victories in his first season with Loomis, a long-time crew chief at Petty Enterprises. Though he won at Talladega, Sears Point and Richmond, Gordon had not finished a season with fewer than seven victories since 1994, his second year with Hendrick Motorsports. His ninth-place finish in points was his worst since a 14th in 1993.

In 2001, however, Gordon silenced the skeptics who had failed to take sufficient notice of his own prodigious talent

## STATS (SINCE 1997)

| YEAR | STARTS | WINS | TOP 5 | TOP 10 | MONEY |
|---|---|---|---|---|---|
| 2001 | 36 | 6 | 18 | 24 | $10,879,757 |
| 2000 | 34 | 3 | 11 | 22 | $3,001,144 |
| 1999 | 34 | 7 | 18 | 21 | $5,858,633 |
| 1998 | 33 | 13 | 26 | 28 | $9,306,584 |
| 1997 | 32 | 10 | 22 | 23 | $6,375,658 |
| CAREER | 293 | 58 | 147 | 190 | $45,748,580 |

behind the wheel. The season brought not only a fourth Winston Cup title for Gordon but also a variety of other significant milestones. He claimed six victories, including an unprecedented third win in the Brickyard 400. He won for the first time at Las Vegas and captured the inaugural event at Kansas City, bringing the number of different racetracks on which he had scored at least one victory to 20.

Gordon won $10,879,757 in prize money, breaking the record of $9,306,584 he set in 1998. He passed the late Dale Earnhardt for the lead in career earnings, heading the all-time list with $45,748,580. In 2001, he led 2,320 laps—more than twice the total of any other driver. At age 30, Gordon became the youngest driver to win four championships.

Suddenly, Gordon's detractors were touting his chances to equal or break the record seven Winston Cup titles shared by Richard Petty and Earnhardt. For Gordon, though, winning was nothing new. It was expected.

The Vallejo, California, native had been driving race cars since kindergarten. In 1979, at age eight, he won his first national championship in quarter midgets. After winning the 1990 USAC Midget title, he moved from open-wheeled cars to NASCAR's Busch Series. Gordon was Rookie of the Year on stock car racing's junior circuit in

**24**

Birthdate: August 4, 1971
Birthplace: Vallejo, CA
Team: Hendrick Motorsports
Sponsor: DuPont
Owner: Rick Hendrick
Crew Chief: Robbie Loomis
Car: Chevrolet

**In a snowstorm of confetti, Jeff Gordon exults in his fourth Winston Cup championship.**

# Jeff **GORDON**

1991, but he still had time to capture the USAC Silver Crown championship that same season.

In 1992, he won three races and a series-record 11 poles driving a Busch car. That was all the seasoning he needed to begin his meteoric rise to the top of the Winston Cup standings. His first full season in Winston Cup was auspicious; though he failed to win a race in 1993, Gordon captured his first Winston Cup pole at Charlotte and posted seven top-five finishes.

The following season brought a pair of victories in two of stock car racing's most prestigious events—the Coca-Cola 600 at Charlotte and the inaugural Brickyard 400 at Indianapolis. After those two wins came the deluge, which culminated in the championship run of 1998, when Gordon tied Petty's modern-era record of 13 victories in a single

## I think I've become a smarter race car driver.

season. (The "modern era" dates to 1972, the first year of Winston's sponsorship of NASCAR's foremost series.)

With 58 career victories, Gordon is the leader among active drivers in that category. To put that accomplishment into perspective, consider that he is comfortably ahead of drivers who have been competing in Winston Cup since the mid-1970s—Bill Elliott, Ricky Rudd and his own teammate, Terry Labonte. Rusty Wallace, who made his Winston Cup debut in 1980, is second on the list with 54 wins and is the only other active driver with more than 41.

Gordon believes his uncanny ability to communicate the handling characteristics on his No. 24 Chevrolet is crucial to the team's success.

"I don't think that my skills as a driver have gotten better," Gordon said. "I think I just have gotten better at communicating and knowing what I need the car to do over a 500-mile race… I think I've become a smarter race car driver. I try to analyse every track that we go to, every situation we've been in, and learn from it."

**Jeff Gordon is as comfortable in a night race at Bristol as on the banks of a superspeedway or the tight corners of a road course.**

# Bobby HAMILTON

**Bobby Hamilton's career came full circle in 1996 at the Phoenix International Raceway. It was there that Hamilton earned the first of his four Winston Cup victories, when his Pontiac outran Mark Martin's Ford to the checkered flag.**

It was at Phoenix, too, that Hamilton got his start in Winston Cup racing seven years earlier, when he drove a car owned by Paramount Pictures and prepared by Hendrick Motorsports in a race used for action footage in the Tom Cruise movie *Days of Thunder*. A short-track star who enjoyed a formidable reputation in Nashville, Tennessee (his home town), Hamilton surprised NASCAR's elite drivers with a fifth-place qualifying effort in his debut.

(Perhaps least surprised was former series champion Darrell Waltrip, who had recommended Hamilton for the job. Hamilton had beaten Winston Cup veterans Waltrip, Sterling Marlin and Bill Elliott in a four-car "Superstar Showdown" at Nashville Speedway in 1988.)

Hamilton twice led the Phoenix race and was running tenth when he parked the No. 51 Chevrolet on lap 215. Officially, Hamilton's exit from the "Autoworks 500" was listed as a "DNF" for engine failure. In reality, NASCAR forced him to retire from the race—after all, drivers of the "movie cars" were not regular competitors in the Winston Cup Series.

Two years later, Hamilton won 1991 Winston Cup Rookie of the Year honors in George Bradshaw's No. 68 Tri-Star Motorsports Oldsmobile and finished 22nd in the points standings. Five years and four car owners later, he won for the first time at Phoenix, in the famous powder-blue livery of Petty Enterprises.

In the fall of 1997, he won at Rockingham, his last victory in the Petty colors. Driving the No. 4 Kodak Chevy for Morgan-McClure Motorsports in 1998, he notched his third

career win at Martinsville. Winless in his next two seasons with Morgan McClure, Hamilton joined Andy Petree's operation for the 2001 season and gave Petree his first victory as a car owner in the Talladega 500.

But Hamilton's career has been plagued by inconsistency. In 2000, he failed to finish 11 races—a high watermark for futility in the series that year. In 2001, despite the win at Talladega and a career-best $2,527,310 in prize money, he finished 18th in points.

For Hamilton, the 2002 season started as an uneven affair. After finishing 33rd in the season-opening Daytona 500, Hamilton improved to ninth at one of his favorite tracks—Rockingham—in the second race of the campaign.

Getting comfortable with first-year crew chief Charley Pressley is essential to an improved position in 2002. The Rockingham race was encouraging.

"I was really impressed with the communication between the teams and the way me and Charley talked things through," Hamilton said. "We pulled a few tricks out of our sleeves at the end and held on for a strong top-ten finish. It was a pretty good day for us."

Hamilton is convinced it will not be the last. After all, his Winston Cup debut was right from a movie script—literally—and Hamilton is still auditioning for the lead role.

## STATS (SINCE 1997)

| YEAR | STARTS | WINS | TOP 5 | TOP 10 | MONEY |
|------|--------|------|-------|--------|-------|
| 2001 | 36 | 1 | 3 | 7 | $2,527,310 |
| 2000 | 34 | 0 | 0 | 2 | $1,619,775 |
| 1999 | 34 | 0 | 1 | 10 | $2,019,255 |
| 1998 | 33 | 1 | 3 | 8 | $2,089,566 |
| 1997 | 32 | 1 | 6 | 8 | $1,478,843 |
| **CAREER** | **337** | **4** | **20** | **64** | **$12,990,059** |

## 55

Birthdate: May 29, 1957
Birthplace: Nashville, TN
Team: Andy Petree Racing
Sponsor: Schneider Electric
Owner: Andy Petree
Crew Chief: Charley Pressley
Car: Chevrolet

*Bobby Hamilton needs to solve the riddle of his team's inconsistent performances.*

# Kevin HARVICK

**Kevin Harvick's breakthrough opportunity in Winston Cup racing wasn't supposed to happen when it did. The idea was not to rush the prodigous driver into the big time.**

But the death of Dale Earnhardt on the final lap of the Daytona 500 on February 18, 2001 forced Harvick into the fray much earlier than car owner Richard Childress had planned.

Harvick had intended to run for the championship in NASCAR's Busch Series, but when the Winston Cup drivers took the green flag for the second race of the year at Rockingham, Harvick was behind the wheel of Childress' No. 29 Chevrolet. (In deference to Earnhardt, the No. 3 was retired indefinitely).

Thus began one of the most remarkable seasons in the history of stock car racing. Harvick went to Victory Lane in his third Winston Cup start, in a photo finish over Jeff Gordon at Atlanta Motor Speedway. No other driver in the modern era (1972 to date) has posted a win that soon after his debut.

Harvick wasn't finished. He won the inaugural Winston Cup race at Chicagoland Speedway and ended the season ninth in the points standings, despite his absence from the Daytona 500. The next highest finish by a driver who did not run all 36 races was 25th (Robert Pressley).

And by the way, Harvick still managed to compete in the Busch Series, despite a schedule that often forced him to fly back and forth between races when Busch and Winston Cup did not hold companion events. Despite the problems inherent in qualifying and practicing in cars in two different series, Harvick nevertheless was strong enough to win the Busch title, backing up his Rookie of the Year performance of 2000.

All told, counting one start in the Craftsman Truck Series, Harvick competed in 70 events at 30 different racetracks. In all of his racing endeavors combined, he covered more than 20,000 miles. Sweetening his remarkable rookie season was prize money totalling more than $4.5 million.

There were those who felt that Harvick's iron-man performances under adverse circumstances in 2001 merited consideration for Driver of the Year honors, but Harvick gives most of the credit to his car owner and the Childress organization.

"As far as the Driver of the Year stuff," Harvick said, "there are a lot of drivers that deserve Driver of the Year, but I think, if we had a Driver and Team of the Year award, it would go to Richard Childress Racing for sure for everything they went through. They've obviously been dealt a hand that was probably the toughest circumstance for Richard Childress to put himself or anybody else into. If he had said, 'Yeah, I'm going to take a year off and not do this for a year and think about whether I'm going to again,' everybody would have understood. Instead he stood right in there, flew back and forth with me across the country, and we did everything we needed to do to make it the best possible situation we could. So I think RCR is an organization that deserves that credit."

And it was Harvick's relationship with Childress that helped carry both owner and driver through a difficult season.

"Richard has done a lot for me in my career," Harvick said. "Basically, I was struggling in the Craftsman Truck Series to make a name for myself. Richard came out of nowhere and put me in his car in the Busch Series, and obviously when everything happened, I told him, 'You do whatever you think is right, and I'm going to stand you behind you 100 per cent.' That's what he did for me. It's not

| | |
|---|---|
| **29** | Birthdate: December 8, 1975 |
| | Birthplace: Bakersfield, CA |
| | Team: Richard Childress Racing |
| | Sponsor: GM Goodwrench Service |
| | Owner: Richard Childress |
| | Crew Chief: Kevin Hamlin |
| | Car: Chevrolet |

**Kevin Harvick won the Atlanta race in March of 2001 in his third Winston Cup start.**

like going to a job where you go and say, 'Well, this is not in my contract,' because the fact of the matter is, we didn't even have a contract, and that didn't matter. I told him, 'We can do whatever it takes to make it all happen.'"

Though Harvick's ability to adapt to a Winston Cup car seemed uncanny, those who had followed his career—including Childress—were not unduly surprised by his success. A Go-Kart racer since age five, Harvick won seven

## "I told him, 'We can do whatever it takes to make it all happen'. "

national karting titles and two Grand National championships before climbing behind the wheel of a late model stock car. In 1993, at age 18, he won the track championship at Mesa Marin Raceway in Bakersfield, California, his home town.

Harvick's fast track to the Winston Cup scene included a Rookie of the Year crown in the Featherlite Southwest Series (1995), a Winston West championship (1998) and 11 top-ten finishes in his first season in the Truck Series (1999).

And lest we forget, 2001 was a banner year for Harvick in another sense—he married wife DeLana in Las Vegas two days after his Winston Cup debut at Rockingham.

**Kevin Harvick grabbed his NASCAR chance with both hands.**

## STATS (SINCE 1997)

| YEAR | STARTS | WINS | TOP 5 | TOP 10 | MONEY |
|---|---|---|---|---|---|
| 2001 | 35 | 2 | 6 | 16 | 4,302,202 |
| 2000 | did not compete | | | | |
| 1999 | did not compete | | | | |
| 1998 | did not compete | | | | |
| 1997 | did not compete | | | | |
| TOTAL | 35 | 2 | 6 | 16 | 4,302,202 |

# Dale **JARRETT**

**If the current roster of NASCAR superstars is heavily populated with "child prodigies"—Jeff Gordon, Tony Stewart and Kevin Harvick come to mind—you can count second-generation driver Dale Jarrett among the late bloomers, a somewhat surprising turn of events considering his pedigree.**

The son of two-time Winston Cup champion Ned Jarrett, Dale didn't settle on a racing career during his teenage years, as had been the case with other notable sons of famous fathers (Richard and Kyle Petty, for instance). Instead, Jarrett played football, basketball and golf at Newton-Conover High School near his home town of Hickory, North Carolina—and he played them all extremely well. Jarrett was all-conference in all three sports and was accomplished enough at golf to consider a career as a professional. The University of South Carolina offered him full golf scholarship, which Jarrett declined.

The lure of racing finally overshadowed his affinity for other sports after Jarrett began driving limited sportsman cars at historic Hickory Motor Speedway in 1977, at age 20. He continued to make a name for himself in late model stocks until NASCAR revamped its Late Model Sportsman division as the Busch Series in 1982.

But success in the Busch Series (he has 11 victories and 14 poles to his credit) didn't translate immediately to success in the Winston Cup. Jarrett's early years in NASCAR's elite series were almost pedestrian—in other words, he might as well have been walking. Driving sporadically for eight different car owners from 1984 through 1988—in equipment that was less than state-of-the-art—he failed to post a top-five finish in his first 57 starts.

After a 1989 season that produced two fifth-place finishes for owner Cale Yarborough, Jarrett signed on with the Wood Brothers in 1990. A year later, three months shy of his 35th birthday, Jarrett claimed his first Winston Cup victory in the Champion 400 at Michigan.

The improved results of 1991 (two poles and a 17th-place finish in points to go with the win) provided the springboard Jarrett needed to land a ride with the rookie team of Joe Gibbs, former coach of the Super Bowl champion Washington Redskins of the National Football League.

After a 1992 season that produced two top-fives and eight top-tens, Jarrett accounted for one of NASCAR's most unforgettable moments in the Daytona 500 of 1993. With his father calling the race from the television broadcast booth—and unable to contain his excitement—Jarrett edged Dale Earnhardt for the victory. Though he failed to win another race that season, Jarrett nevertheless posted 13 top-fives en route to his highest finish in the points thus far—fourth.

His third year with Gibbs was his last, but Jarrett did notch another victory in the fall 1994 race at Charlotte. It was the following season, however, that would bring the association that would allow Jarrett to realize his full potential as a driver.

With his regular driver, Ernie Irvan, unable to compete because of a career-threatening injury suffered during a practice crash at Michigan, car owner Robert Yates hired Jarrett to drive the No. 28 Ford in 1995. Jarrett won at Pocono, Pennsylvania, and finished third in points in his first season with Yates.

In 1996, Jarrett switched car numbers—to Yates' No. 88 Ford—and found a home. With crew chief Todd Parrott

**Dale Jarrett reached the pinnacle of his career with a Winston Cup championship in 1999.**

Birthdate: November 26, 1956

Birthplace: Newton, NC

Team: Robert Yates Racing

Sponsor: YOS

Owner: Robert Yates

Crew Chief: Todd Parrott

Car: Ford

## Dale **JARRETT**

making the calls in the pits, Jarrett claimed four more victories, including his second Daytona 500 and the prestigious Brickyard 400 at Indianapolis. The following season brought seven victories, a second-place finish in points and Jarrett's selection as Driver of the Year by the National Motorsports Press Association.

But 1999 was the pinnacle of Jarrett's career. He won four races on the way to his first Winston Cup champi-

## "The competition is closer, and that keeps your adrenaline going..."

onship, at age 42. In doing so, Dale and Ned Jarrett became only the second father-son combination to win the series title, following Lee and Richard Petty. Jarrett backed up his championship season with two wins in 2000 and four more in 2001.

Though his 45th birthday is behind him, Jarrett doesn't see retirement in his immediate future.

"I can only look back to Dale Earnhardt," Jarrett said. "He was still winning and very competitive [at age 49] and may have been on the verge of having another one of his better years before he was taken from us. I think that guys now are in better shape. Obviously, the competition is closer, and that keeps your adrenaline going a little bit."

**Dale Jarrett remains as competitive as ever even in his 46th year.**

## STATS (SINCE 1997)

| YEAR | STARTS | WINS | TOP 5 | TOP 10 | MONEY |
|------|--------|------|-------|--------|-------|
| 2001 | 36 | 4 | 12 | 19 | $5,377,742 |
| 2000 | 34 | 2 | 15 | 24 | $5,934,475 |
| 1999 | 34 | 4 | 24 | 29 | $6,649,596 |
| 1998 | 33 | 3 | 19 | 22 | $4,019,657 |
| 1997 | 32 | 7 | 20 | 23 | $3,240,542 |
| **CAREER** | **459** | **28** | **141** | **210** | **$33,274,832** |

# Jimmie JOHNSON

**A relative late-comer to stock car racing after gaining a wealth of "off-road" experience, Jimmie Johnson turned out to be the early bird when it came to advancing his Winston Cup career.**

In his first full season in the Busch Series (2000), Johnson turned the heads of several Winston Cup owners with a tenth-place finish in the points. With a variety of opportunities opening up for him, Johnson went to Jeff Gordon for career advice in August of that year.

As it turned out, Gordon and Rick Hendrick had decided to start a fourth racing team, with Gordon as co-owner. Johnson was one of a handful of drivers they were considering, but Johnson's conversation with Gordon accelerated the process.

"To my surprise, he was interested and Rick Hendrick was interested in trying a fourth team, and all of a sudden, they're looking at me as being their driver," Johnson said. "… I think probably in a few months' to six months' time, they would have approached me… When I came to them with my situation, it kind of sped up the process, and it just made it all happen sooner. I think I would have been approached eventually, but it was destiny when I went to them as early as I did, and they reacted as they did."

Before he got his first taste of the Busch Series in 1998, Johnson was far more comfortable driving a truck on any surface other than asphalt. For three straight years, 1992–94, he won the Mickey Thompson Stadium championship. In 1994, he also won the SCORE Desert Championship, and in 1996 and 1997 he claimed the SODA Winter Series title. In 1998, the same year he entered his first three Busch races, he also won Rookie of the Year honors in the ASA ACDelco Challenge Series.

## STATS (SINCE 1997)

| YEAR | STARTS | WINS | TOP 5 | TOP 10 | MONEY |
|------|--------|------|-------|--------|-------|
| 2001 | 3 | 0 | 0 | 0 | 122,320 |
| 2000 | did not compete | | | | |
| 1999 | did not compete | | | | |
| 1998 | did not compete | | | | |
| 1997 | did not compete | | | | |
| **TOTAL** | **3** | **0** | **0** | **0** | **122,320** |

It wasn't until 2001 that Johnson won his first Busch Series race, the inaugural event at Chicagoland Speedway. With nine top-ten results that season, he finished eighth in points. Johnson also competed in three Winston Cup races in 2001; in his debut at Charlotte he qualified 15th—a clear portent of the strong efforts that were to come.

The start to his 2002 Winston Cup rookie season couldn't have been better. Driving for Hendrick and Gordon, Johnson won the pole for the season-opening Daytona 500. But Johnson is one to temper his desire to win with a patient attitude.

"The racer inside of us wants to be competitive out of the box," Johnson said. "We have high expectations of ourselves, but we are not going to let the pressure of performing allow us make bad decisions or force the issue. We are going to try to get into an environment so I can grow and develop as a driver at my own pace. We're all hoping it is sooner rather than later."

Those hopes were justified. In the ninth race of the 2002 season, Johnson won his second pole of the year and finished seventh in the Aaron's 499 at Talladega. A week later he notched the first Winston Cup victory of his burgeoning career at Fontana, California.

**Jimmie Johnson joined the list of Winston Cup rookie winners in 2002.**

## 48

Birthdate: September 17, 1975

Birthplace: El Cajon, CA

Team: Hendrick Motorsports

Sponsor: Lowe's

Owners: Rick Hendrick, Jeff Gordon

Crew Chief: Chad Knaus

Car: Chevrolet

# Matt KENSETH

**Perhaps the greatest compliment to a teacher is for a student to surpass his mentor's level of accomplishment. It may be time for Matt Kenseth to do just that.**

Winston Cup veteran Mark Martin first took notice of Kenseth's formidable talent during a Busch Series race at Talladega, Alabama. Since then, the two drivers have enjoyed a solid friendship born of mutual respect. Martin helped teach Kenseth the nuances of big-time stock car racing, and now Kenseth appears ready to become a big-time star in his own right.

It was no surprise that Kenseth's name would rise to the top of the list in 1999, when owner Jack Roush (who has fielded cars for Martin since 1988) wanted to expand his operation. And it wasn't simply that Martin lobbied earnestly on his young friend's behalf.

Kenseth had already shown his mettle in 1998 as a substitute driver for Bill Elliott, who missed a race while attending his father's funeral. Kenseth drove Elliott's No. 94 Ford to a sixth-place finish at the difficult "Monster Mile" in Dover, Delaware—a remarkable accomplishment for his first "seat time" in a Winston Cup car.

A full-time competitor in the Busch Series in 1999, Kenseth also competed in five Cup events for Roush, and Dover was again the high watermark of the season. Kenseth posted a fourth-place finish there, his first career top-five in NASCAR's top series.

In 2000, his first full season of Winston Cup racing, Kenseth won the series' longest race, the Coca-Cola 600 at Charlotte. He also won Rookie of the Year honors—a victory that wasn't entirely popular in some quarters, given that the taciturn Kenseth edged out the flamboyant and charismatic Dale Earnhardt Jr. for the rookie crown.

## STATS (SINCE 1996)

| YEAR | STARTS | WINS | TOP 5 | TOP 10 | MONEY |
|---|---|---|---|---|---|
| 2001 | 36 | 0 | 4 | 9 | $2,565,579 |
| 2000 | 34 | 1 | 4 | 11 | $2,408,138 |
| 1999 | 5 | 0 | 1 | 1 | $143,561 |
| 1998 | 1 | 0 | 0 | 1 | $42,340 |
| 1997 | did not compete | | | | |
| **CAREER** | **76** | **1** | **9** | **22** | **$5,159,618** |

But it should be no knock against Kenseth that he is all business on the track. During his rookie season, he finished tenth in the season-opening Daytona 500 and went on to record ten more top-tens before the end of the campaign. It was that level of consistency that allowed him to stay ahead of Earnhardt Jr. in the rookie standings. Overall, Kenseth finished 14th in points.

He improved one position in 2001, a year in which the entire Roush organization lost ground to the rest of the top teams. Nevertheless, Kenseth posted nine top-tens and earned $2,565,579 in prize money. He had three fourth-place finishes—at Michigan, Talladega and Phoenix—but nothing better.

Early in 2002, however, Kenseth found a cure for his winless season of 2001. In February, he won at Rockingham, the same track where he notched his first Busch Series victory in 1998.

Despite his disappointing sophomore season, Kenseth entered 2002 with his pit crew essentially intact, the same group that won the pit crew championship in record time at the fall race at Rockingham. Perhaps that continuity helped ensure the early win in 2002.

"I thought our guys did a good job of preparing our cars [in 2001]," Kenseth said. "We had almost no mechanical failures. That was another part throughout the year where we felt like we were really happy with all our guys."

**Birthdate:** April 10, 1972
**Birthplace:** Cambridge, WI
**Team:** Andy Rousch Racing
**Sponsor:** DeWalt Power Tools
**Owners:** Jack Rousch, Mark Martin
**Crew Chief:** Robbie Reiser
**Car:** Ford

**Matt Kenseth celebrates victory at Rockingham.**

# Bobby LABONTE

**Which "brother act" is the most successful in the history of Winston Cup racing? You could argue the point, because here are many famous names that could deserve the accolade.**

You could make a case for Tim, Fonty and Bob Flock, who totalled 63 victories between them in the early days of NASCAR.

Bobby and Donnie Allison could lay a strong claim to that distinction. Bobby himself accounted for 84 wins and a championship in 1983, while Donnie added ten victories to the family record book. On four occasions when Donnie took the checkered flag, Bobby was right behind him in second place.

But Bobby Labonte's Winston Cup championship in 2000 was unprecedented—with that title, he and brother Terry Labonte (a two-time champion) became the only pair of brothers ever to win NASCAR's most coveted prize.

Bobby Labonte was a quick study. When brother Terry was driving for Billy Hagan during the mid-1980s, Bobby was a member of the crew. Together they celebrated Terry's first Winston Cup championship in 1984.

In 1987, Bobby took a job with car builder Jay Hedgecock. On the weekends he raced late model stock cars at Caraway Speedway in Asheboro, North Carolina. Working on his own cars, he won 12 races and the track title in 1987.

Gradually, Labonte worked his way into the Busch Series. In 1990 he ran the full Busch Grand National schedule for the first time and finished fourth in the points race. A year later he won the Busch title.

The 1991 season also marked Labonte's first foray into Winston Cup racing—he competed in two events in his own car and failed to finish in either. The $8,350 he won for

those first two starts was a far cry from the millions that awaited him later in the decade.

Labonte was absent from Winston Cup in 1992, when he finished three points behind Joe Nemechek in the closest contest for the Busch championship in series history—after he and Todd Bodine rescued Nemechek from a burning car during the season-opening race at Daytona.

When he returned to NASCAR's top series in 1993, Labonte ran a full schedule for owner Bill Davis. Though winless in two seasons for Davis, Labonte claimed his first Winston Cup pole position in the fall 1993 race at Richmond, Virginia.

In 1995, Labonte began the association with owner Joe Gibbs that would eventually lead to the championship in 2000. In each of his first eight seasons with Gibbs, since taking over the No. 18 Interstate Batteries car from Dale Jarrett, Labonte won at least one race and accumulated 18 career victories by the end of 2001. Though eight years younger than Terry, who was born in 1956—and though he made his Winston Cup debut 13 years after Terry's in 1978—Bobby is closing fast on his brother's total of 21 wins through 2001.

Labonte's most prolific year in terms of visits to Victory Lane came in 1999, when he finished second in the title race to Dale Jarrett. Labonte won five times that season—at Dover, at Pocono twice, at Michigan and at Atlanta. During his championship season a year later, he cemented his claim to the title with an early win at Rockingham, his first victory in the Brickyard 400 at Indianapolis, his first victory in the Southern 500 at Darlington, and an emphatic win in the October race at Charlotte.

As is often the case after the euphoria of a championship season, Labonte's defense of his title got off to an

**18**

Birthdate: May 8, 1964
Birthplace: Corpus Christi, TH
Team: Joe Gibbs Racing
Sponsor: Interstate Batteries
Owner: Joe Gibbs
Crew Chief: Jimmy Makar
Car: Pontiac

**Bobby Labonte drove the No. 18 Pontiac to the Winston Cup championship in 2000.**

extremely slow start. Seven races into the 2001 season, he stood 25th in points, but Labonte rallied during the latter portion of the year to finish sixth. He posted two victories after the season's mid-point at two of his favorite tracks— Pocono and Atlanta.

Labonte is quick to share the credit for his success with crew chief Jimmy Makar, who has called the shots in the pits during each of Labonte's seasons with Gibbs.

## ...whenever he decides to quit, I'm going to quit, too.

"I've never seen a more determined man about racing," Labonte says of Makar. "Our relationship goes back a long way, and we've become great friends over the past years, and we've kind of set up that whenever he decides to quit, I'm going to quit, too."

Perhaps that retirement won't come until Labonte has rewritten the record book with yet another outstanding season. He and Terry could become the first pair of brothers ever to win two championships each.

No wonder then that the city fathers of Corpus Christi, Texas, decided in 2001 to name a park in honor of the two native sons.

**Bobby Labonte's outstanding talent has seen him earn close on $26 million; he has picked almost the same amount of money as his brother Terry, but from 400 fewer races.**

## STATS (SINCE 1996)

| YEAR | STARTS | WINS | TOP 5 | TOP 10 | MONEY |
|------|--------|------|-------|--------|-------|
| 2001 | 36 | 2 | 9 | 20 | $4,786,779 |
| 2000 | 34 | 4 | 19 | 24 | $7,361,386 |
| 1999 | 34 | 5 | 23 | 26 | $4,763,615 |
| 1998 | 33 | 2 | 11 | 18 | $2,980,052 |
| 1997 | 32 | 1 | 9 | 18 | $2,217,999 |
| CAREER | 294 | 18 | 84 | 142 | $25,953,024 |

# Terry LABONTE

**"Texas" Terry Labonte is known as the Iron Man of Winston Cup racing for a good reason. His 655 consecutive starts, spanning more than 20 years, constitute a series record that's in no danger of being broken any time soon.**

And it's not that Labonte simply "turned laps" in those 655 races, before his streak was broken at Indianapolis in 2000. His career has included 21 victories, 26 poles and a pair of championships.

Labonte got an early start on his lengthy career. At age seven, he began racing quarter midgets in his native Texas. In 1978, as an unheralded 21 year old, he landed a ride with car owner Billy Hagan for the Southern 500 at Darlington. Winston Cup veterans were surprised when Labonte qualified 19th for the prestigious race. When he drove Hagan's Chevrolet to a fourth-place finish, they were dumbfounded.

Labonte won $9,850 for his remarkable showing that Sunday. By the end of 2001, his career earnings had exceeded $25 million.

The 1978 Southern 500 began an association with Hagan that lasted nine years. Never a prolific winner on the Winston Cup circuit, Labonte posted his first victory in the 1980 Southern 500 at Darlington, appropriately enough. All told, he won six races for Hagan before signing with Junior Johnson for the 1987 season.

Labonte's tenure with Hagan also included the first of his series titles, in 1984. Though he won but two races that season, at Riverside, California and Bristol, Tennessee, Labonte was the model of consistency. He had six seconds and six thirds to go with the two victories.

Labonte won four races for Johnson before changing owners again in 1990. Winless with Richard Jackson that season, Labonte returned to Hagan in 1991, but the drought continued for three years. It wasn't until Labonte accepted a ride from Rick Hendrick in 1994 that his fortunes took a turn for the better.

He won three times that season, at now-defunct North Wilkesboro, Richmond and Phoenix. A year later he matched that career-best mark for victories in a season with wins at Richmond, Pocono and Bristol.

The third season with Hendrick brought two victories—and a second championship. The 12-year span between the first and second titles is a record for the Winston Cup Series. It was also in 1996 that Labonte eclipsed Richard Petty's record of 514 consecutive starts.

Three-and-a-half years later, injuries suffered in a violent crash in the Pepsi 400 at Daytona forced Labonte to miss the Brickyard 400, and the streak ended at 655 races. For the first year since 1993, and for the first since he joined Hendrick Motorsports, Labonte failed to win a race.

But if 2000 was a disappointing season, 2001 was worse. Despite competing in all 36 points events, Labonte failed to lead a single lap. Nevertheless, he continues to scoff at the notion that his career is over. With the new crew chief Jim Long on board for 2002 in place of Gary DeHart, Labonte has reason for optimism.

## STATS (SINCE 1997)

| YEAR | STARTS | WINS | TOP 5 | TOP 10 | MONEY |
|---|---|---|---|---|---|
| 2001 | 36 | 0 | 1 | 3 | $3,011,901 |
| 2000 | 32 | 0 | 3 | 6 | $2,239,716 |
| 1999 | 34 | 1 | 1 | 7 | $2,475,365 |
| 1998 | 33 | 1 | 5 | 15 | $2,054,163 |
| 1997 | 32 | 1 | 8 | 20 | $2,270,144 |
| CAREER | 709 | 21 | 176 | 340 | $26,536,692 |

**5**

Birthdate: November 16, 1956
Birthplace: Corpus Christi, TX
Team: Hendrick Motorsports
Sponsor: Kellogg's
Owner: Rick Hendrick
Crew Chief: Jim Long
Car: Chevrolet

**Texas Terry Labonte is the "Iron Man" of Winston Cup racing.**

# Sterling MARLIN

**If ever a driver defied conventional wisdom in 2001, that driver was Sterling Marlin. The veteran from Tennessee wasn't expected to be the key player in one of the stories of the NASCAR season.**

After all, Bill Elliott and Casey Atwood were supposed to be at the vanguard of Dodge's triumphant return to Winston Cup racing, in cars fielded by Ray Evernham with the backing and blessing of the Chrysler Corporation.

But it was Marlin, a restrictor-plate racing specialist, who led the parade, driving for a team revitalized by the advent of vaunted IndyCar owner Chip Ganassi, who had purchased a controlling interest in Felix Sabates' SABCO organization.

With Ganassi at the helm, Marlin ended four years of famine with a victory at Michigan in August—the first win for a Dodge since the late Neil Bonnett took the checkered flag at Ontario, California, on November 20, 1977. Marlin followed this with a victory in the October race at Charlotte, and his third-place finish in the championship standings was the best among the Dodge drivers in 2001. With more than $4.5 million in prize money, Marlin more than doubled his previous best season in the earnings category ($2.253 million in 1995). His 12 top-five finishes were a testament to the quality of the Ganassi organization.

The son of former Winston Cup driver Coo Coo Marlin, Sterling got his start in the series in 1976 at Nashville Raceway, his home track. Substituting for his father, who was sidelined with a broken shoulder, Marlin failed to finish the race.

All told, in a career that has spanned more than a quarter-century, Marlin has driven Winston Cup cars for 16 different owners. His first full season on the circuit didn't come until 1983, when he won Rookie of the Year honors driving for Roger Hamby—though he posted just one top-ten result in 30 races.

It took Marlin eight more years to win his first pole—in a car fielded by Junior Johnson. In 1992 he won five poles, starting in front for both Daytona races and the second event at Talladega, thereby establishing himself as a contender on NASCAR's two restrictor-plate superspeedways.

It wasn't until 1994, however, that Marlin won his first race—appropriately enough, the season-opening Daytona 500. That was his first appearance with the Morgan-McClure Racing team, whose prowess at building restrictor-plate engines meshed perfectly with Marlin's ability to drive the cars.

The Daytona 500 gave Marlin his only victory of 1994, but as if to prove it was no accident, he repeated the feat the following year and joined Richard Petty (1973–74) and Cale Yarborough (1983–84) as the only drivers to win NASCAR's most important race in consecutive years. Marlin's third-place finish in the 1995 points standings was also a career-best. Before the season was over, he added victories at Darlington and Talladega to his Daytona 500 win.

Before leaving Morgan-McClure after the 1997 season, Marlin won twice more—in the 1996 Pepsi 400 at Daytona and the 1996 Talladega 500. The three years that followed his departure must have seemed like purgatory to the veteran driver. With Sabates, Marlin posted just three top-fives in three seasons, and his best finish in the points was 13th in 1998.

Enter Ganassi and the new alliance with Dodge. That

Birthdate: June 30, 1957
Birthplace: Franklin, TN
Team: Chip Ganassi Racing
Sponsor: Coors Light
Owners: Chip Ganassi, Felix Sabates
Crew Chief: Lee McCall
Car: Dodge

**Sterling Marlin gets some last-minute advice before firing the engine in his No. 40 Dodge.**

was all Marlin needed to jump-start his career.

"I think the last few races [of 2001] showed how good we really were," Marlin says. "Chip turned this team around and reorganized the whole place. He hired a lot more people, had Ernie Elliott [Bill Elliott's brother] build our motors, and everything just went real smooth."

"Smooth" is hardly an apt way to describe Marlin's start to the 2002 season. A penalty for pulling a bent fender away from the right-front tire under red-flag conditions may have cost him a win at the Daytona 500, and a yellow-flag finish deprived him of a chance to win at Rockingham a week later.

# I think the last few races [of 2001] showed how good we really were.

But Marlin benefited from a lack of radio communication between NASCAR officials at the season's third race at Las Vegas, when NASCAR tried to impose a 15-second penalty on him for speeding on the pit road, then rescinded when the official in the pits failed to hold the car.

Marlin won the race, and after four events he found himself in an uncharacteristic position—on top of the points standings. Perhaps his ship is ready to arrive.

**Sparks fly from Sterling Marlin's Dodge.**

## STATS (SINCE 1997)

| YEAR | STARTS | WINS | TOP 5 | TOP 10 | MONEY |
|------|--------|------|-------|--------|-------|
| 2001 | 36 | 2 | 12 | 20 | $4,517,634 |
| 2000 | 34 | 0 | 1 | 7 | $1,992,301 |
| 1999 | 34 | 0 | 2 | 5 | $1,797,416 |
| 1998 | 32 | 0 | 0 | 6 | $1,350,161 |
| 1997 | 32 | 0 | 2 | 6 | $1,301,370 |
| CAREER | 539 | 8 | 71 | 178 | $19,899,539 |

# Mark MARTIN

**Though he's hardly considering retirement in his early 40s, Mark Martin has already enjoyed a NASCAR career that places him among the all-time greats of the sport.**

Consider that Martin entered the 2002 season with 32 career Winston Cup victories, tied for 17th on the all-time list with the legendary Glenn "Fireball" Roberts. Consider that Martin has won races on every sort of venue—from the shorts tracks at Richmond, North Wilkesboro and Martinsville to the intermediate speedways at Charlotte and Atlanta to the high banks of Talladega to the road courses at Sears Point (California) and Watkins Glen (New York).

Consider that Martin shattered the record for victories in the Busch Series (he has won 45 races) while competing almost exclusively in companion events that coincided with his Winston Cup schedule.

Consider that Martin won a career-best seven Cup events in 1998, and that from 1989 through 2000, he never finished outside the top ten in the Winston Cup standings.

There is, however, one significant accomplishment Martin would like to add to his resume before he leaves the sport: a Winston Cup championship.

Martin has come tantalizingly close to realizing that dream—never more so than in 1990, when he finished second in the standings, 26 points behind the late Dale Earnhardt. But for a 46-point penalty for a carburetor infraction discovered after Martin's victory at Richmond in February, he might well have won the title that year.

In 1997, Martin was third in the championship race, a mere 29 points behind winner Jeff Gordon, and, in 1998, he was a distant second to Gordon—ever the bridesmaid.

## STATS (SINCE 1997)

| YEAR | STARTS | WINS | TOP 5 | TOP 10 | MONEY |
|---|---|---|---|---|---|
| 2001 | 36 | 0 | 3 | 15 | $3,797,006 |
| 2000 | 34 | 1 | 13 | 20 | $3,098,874 |
| 1999 | 34 | 2 | 19 | 26 | $3,509,744 |
| 1998 | 33 | 7 | 22 | 26 | $4,309,006 |
| 1997 | 32 | 4 | 16 | 24 | $2,532,484 |
| CAREER | 494 | 32 | 188 | 293 | $29,165,322 |

Despite the lack of a title, however, Martin is an Arkansas boy who has arrived in the big-time. But his success didn't come quickly. He started 57 races for seven different owners (including himself), before making the deal that would propel him into the upper echelons of stock car racing. In 1988, he signed on with Jack Roush.

The association is one of uncharacteristic loyalty on both sides. Despite a disappointing 2001, when he failed to win a race for the first time since 1996; despite back problems that have necessitated surgery and limited Martin's ability to pursue daily work-outs in the gym; despite rumblings that the Roush teams were on the decline, Martin and Roush began their 15th season together in 2002.

"We just realigned our people a little bit and realigned our strategy a little bit," Martin said of the No. 6 Viagra Ford team's off-season changes after the 2001 season. "Nothing really earth-shattering. Everybody in the sport works—you can't work harder than the rest of them [other race teams] any more, so hopefully you have to try to work smarter…"

Something must be working. Through the first four races of 2002, all four Roush teams were in the top ten in points—led by Martin in fourth place.

**Mark Martin has won 32 Winston Cup races since joining forces with Jack Roush in 1988.**

6

Birthdate: January 9, 1959
Birthplace: Batesville, AR
Team: Roush Racing
Sponsor: Pfizer/Viagra
Owner: Jack Roush
Crew Chief: Ben Leslie
Car: Ford

# Jeremy MAYFIELD

**No one has ever claimed that Jeremy Mayfield lacks self-assurance. Admirers might call him confident. Detractors might characterize his manner as downright cocky.**

Whatever the label, the brash 32-year-old driver from Kentucky has ample reason to believe in his own abilities. So does car owner Ray Evernham, who took on a third team in 2002—and risked hurting Casey Atwood's feelings—just to make room in his organization for Mayfield.

Though Mayfield had just three victories to his credit in nine years on the Winston Cup circuit, Evernham thought enough of the young driver to put him behind the wheel of the No. 19 Dodge, moving Atwood (a rookie in 2001) to the No. 7 team Evernham co-owns with Jim Smith.

There's only one catch to the new arrangement. Now Mayfield will have to prove himself.

A driver who developed his skills in late model stock cars and the touring ARCA Series, Mayfield made his Winston Cup debut at Charlotte in October 1993; he started 30th and finished 29th—ten laps down—in Earl Sadler's No. 95 Ford.

In 1994, he drove four times for Sadler, four times for T.W. Taylor and 12 times for former Winston Cup champion Cale Yarborough. By his own admission, Yarborough did not have the finances to put top-quality equipment on the track, and Mayfield managed just two top-five results during his two-year tenure with the only driver to win three straight Winston Cup championships.

The 1996 season brought one of the most interesting "deals" in the history of NASCAR racing. Though it wasn't a "trade" in the same sense as a swap of baseball players, Mayfield and John Andretti switched rides two-thirds of the way through the year. Andretti left the Michael Kranefuss team to drive for Yarborough, and Mayfield signed on to drive for Kranefuss.

Though he failed to win in 1997, Mayfield improved his level of performance with three top-fives, eight top-tens and a 13th-place finish in the championship standings. Roger Penske bought into the team before the 1998 season, and, coincidentally or not, Mayfield recorded his first victory in the June race at Pocono, Pennsylvania, and finished seventh in points.

After a winless 1999 season, Mayfield recorded two more wins during an inconsistent 2000 campaign. He won at Fontana, California, in April—on a two-mile superspeedway owned by Penske—and followed that with his second victory at Pocono, where he pulled the "bump-and-run" on the late Dale Earnhardt on the final lap.

"I was just trying to rattle his cage," Mayfield said of the final-lap incident, borrowing Earnhardt's own description of a similar situation between Earnhardt and Terry Labonte at Bristol in August 1999.

Mayfield, however, failed to finish 11 races in 2000, and friction between Mayfield and team-mate Rusty Wallace, the Penske organization's No. 1 driver, was an ill-kept secret. Twenty-eight races into the 2001 season, Mayfield was released by Penske and went off in pursuit of the ride he coveted. The announcement that he would join Evernham came before the end of the year.

"This is what I had hoped for ever since I moved to the Winston Cup Series," Mayfield says. "To have a guy like

## STATS (SINCE 1997)

| YEAR | STARTS | WINS | TOP 5 | TOP 10 | MONEY |
|---|---|---|---|---|---|
| 2001 | 28 | 0 | 5 | 7 | $2,682,603 |
| 2000 | 32 | 2 | 6 | 12 | $2,169,251 |
| 1999 | 34 | 0 | 5 | 12 | $2,125,227 |
| 1998 | 33 | 1 | 12 | 16 | $2,332,034 |
| 1997 | 32 | 0 | 3 | 8 | $1,067,203 |
| CAREER | 237 | 3 | 33 | 58 | $11,637,071 |

**19**

Birthdate: May 27, 1969
Birthplace: Owensboro, KY
Team: Evernham Motorsports
Sponsor: Dodge Dealers/UAW
Owner: Ray Evernham
Crew Chief: Sammy Johns
Car: Dodge

**Jeremy Mayfield posted two of his three career wins in the Mobil 1 Ford.**

Ray Evernham at your side—who pushes you to be your best and then encourages you to give more—is what I've always wanted. He's a true racer in every sense of the word, and I respect him more than anybody.

"I never thought I would actually get to race for him. When he first put his deal together last year we talked, but

I couldn't get out of my contract, and then he hired Casey. I thought it was going to be too late. I thought I had lost my chance, but when Roger (Penske) let go of me the Monday night after Kansas City, Ray called me Tuesday morning and that was the best vote of confidence anyone could have given me."

# Jerry NADEAU

**Jerry Nadeau arrived at the most important event in his racing career—signing a deal to drive for Hendrick Motorsports—by a circuitous route.**

Winner of ten World Karting Association and International Karting Foundation championships between 1984 and 1990, Nadeau had already gained a wide variety of racing experience before he ever tried his hand in a stock car.

He was Skip Barber Eastern Series Rookie of the Year in 1991. From 1993 to 1995 he won nine races in the Skip Barber Pro Series. In 1995 and 1996 he entered seven Busch Series races, but his most impressive accomplishment took place in 1996 in Europe, where he finished sixth in the Formula Opel Series, the best-ever result by an American.

Nadeau's background also includes a go-kart race on ice in St. Petersburg, Russia, where he finished second in 1992.

But his Winston Cup career was a struggle from his first race for owner Richard Jackson in 1997—Nadeau failed to finish two of the five races he entered that year. In 1998—driving 14 races for a team owned by Bill Elliott and Miami Dolphins quarterback Dan Marino, and 16 events for Harry Melling—Nadeau finished third in the Winston Cup Rookie of the Year standings, but failed to post a top-ten in 30 races.

In 1999, Nadeau again switched rides in the middle of the season, moving after 22 events from Melling Racing to the No. 36 Cartoon Network Pontiac owned by Thomas Beard and Nelson Bowers. Nadeau scored the first top-five of his Winston Cup career at Watkins Glen (New York), hardly surprising given his successful history on road courses.

The 2000 season brought the offer from Hendrick as well as Nadeau's first Cup victory. At the end of a roller-coaster season in which he failed to finish nine races, he won the final event of the year at Atlanta, where he crossed the finish line barely more than a second ahead of Dale Earnhardt. In a race delayed for a day by rain, Nadeau was strong all afternoon. He led 155 laps, more than any other driver.

In November 2001, Nadeau appeared certain to duplicate his Atlanta victory. With a four-second lead on the final lap of the NAPA 500, he ran out of fuel and coasted to the finish line in fourth place.

To Nadeau, the two Atlanta races were a microcosm of his career in stock car racing. "It's kind of been my whole life," he said. "My whole career has been up and down. Nothing really ever came easy to me in anything I've ever done… I feel I finally started my career with an operation—with Hendrick Motorsports. I've got a lot to learn, and I'm grateful to be in Winston Cup racing."

As Nadeau looks ahead, however, the 2002 season will necessitate another adjustment. Crew chief Tony Furr resigned from Hendrick Motorsports in April, leaving Ken Howes to direct Nadeau's team from the pit box.

Nadeau matched his best qualifying effort of the year with a fifth at Fontana, California (after Furr's departure), but 10 races into the campaign, the talented young driver was mired in 26th place in the points standings.

## STATS (SINCE 1997)

| YEAR | STARTS | WINS | TOP 5 | TOP 10 | MONEY |
|---|---|---|---|---|---|
| 2001 | 36 | 0 | 4 | 10 | $2,507,827 |
| 2000 | 34 | 1 | 3 | 5 | $2,164,778 |
| 1999 | 34 | 0 | 1 | 2 | $1,370,229 |
| 1998 | 30 | 0 | 0 | 0 | $804,867 |
| 1997 | 5 | 0 | 0 | 0 | $118,545 |
| CAREER | 139 | 1 | 8 | 17 | $6,966,246 |

25

Birthdate: September 9, 1970
Birthplace: Danbury, CT
Team: Hendrick Motorsports
Sponsor: UAW/Delphi
Owner: Joe Hendrick
Crew Chief: Ken Howes
Car: Chevrolet

**The No. 25 pit crew goes to work on Jerry Nadeau's Chevy during a green-flag pit stop.**

# Joe NEMECHEK

**Nicknamed "Front Row Joe" for his prowess in qualifying sessions, Joe Nemechek is still searching for the right showcase for his formidable talents as a driver.**

Nemechek had hoped 2002 was going to be the year. After winning the second race of his Winston Cup career for owner Andy Petree at Rockingham in 2001, Nemechek signed with Carter-Haas Racing for 2002. At Carter-Haas, Nemechek was to team with long-time friend Todd Bodine, or so he thought.

However, the bankruptcy of the team's primary sponsor, Kmart, threw the season into turmoil. Sponsorship money ran out after the second race of 2002, forcing owner Travis Carter to scramble on a week-to-week basis to try and keep his cars on the track. Despite a pole-winning effort at Las Vegas, Bodine's car was parked after the third race, and Nemechek's future with Carter-Haas was clouded with uncertainty.

Nemechek made his Winston Cup debut in 1993 at New Hampshire, the same track that would be the site of his first victory 1999. After competing in three races in his own car and two in a car owned by Morgan-McClure in 1993, Nemechek competed in his first full season of Cup racing for owner Larry Hedrick in 1994. In 1995 and 1996 he again ran a full schedule as an owner/driver. In three subsequent seasons with owner Felix Sabates, he notched a lone victory at New Hampshire before signing with Petree for 2000 .

Nemechek's difficulty in getting to Victory Lane in the Winston Cup series was a new and frustrating experience for the Florida-born driver, who turned 38 in September 2001. Unlike many fellow competitors who started racing go-karts, Nemechek got his first taste of competitive racing

| STATS (SINCE 1997) | | | | | |
|---|---|---|---|---|---|
| YEAR | STARTS | WINS | TOP 5 | TOP 10 | MONEY |
| 2001 | 31 | 1 | 1 | 4 | $2,510,723 |
| 2000 | 34 | 0 | 3 | | 9 | $2,105,041 |
| 1999 | 34 | 1 | 1 | 3 | $1,634,946 |
| 1998 | 32 | 0 | 1 | 4 | $1,343,991 |
| 1997 | 30 | 0 | 0 | 3 | $732,194 |
| CAREER | 253 | 2 | 8 | 32 | $9,868,212 |

on a motorcycle at age 13. Six years of motocross produced more than 300 trophies.

Subsequently, he won Rookie of the Year honors and championships in three different racing divisions in three consecutive years: the Southeastern Mini-Stock Series (1987), the United Stock Car Alliance (1988) and NASCAR's All-Pro Series for late model stock cars (1989).

In 1990, Nemechek won the Rookie of the Year award in the Busch Series, and, in 1992, he claimed the Busch championship. Throughout his Winston Cup career, he has continued to race in a number of Busch Series events, none more dramatic than the season's final race at Homestead, Florida, in 1997. Nemechek triumphed at the same track where his brother John had lost his life in a Craftsman Truck Series race earlier that year.

In 190 Busch Series starts through 2001, Nemechek accumulated nine victories and ten pole positions. As the 2002 season approached, before Kmart's bankruptcy hit the news, Nemechek was optimistic about the move to Carter's team. A career Chevy driver, Nemechek was looking forward to piloting Carter's Ford.

"This is my first opportunity to drive a Ford, and I'm expecting big things," Nemechek said. "You see Dale Jarrett and other guys in these cars, and I know I can run with them."

All Nemechek needs now is a stable situation in which he can back up those words.

**26**

Birthdate: September 26, 1963
Birthplace: Naples, FL
Team: Haas/Carter Motorsports
Sponsor: Checker Auto Parts
Owners: Travis Carter, Carl Haas
Crew Chief: Donnie Wingo
Car: Ford

Perhaps it was the Grinch who tried to steal Joe Nemechek's ride with Haas/Carter Motorsports.

# Ryan NEWMAN

**Where did this guy come from? A rookie, Rusty Wallace's team-mate, and he's second in the Winston Cup points standings five races into the 2002 season?**

It almost seems unfair to the myriad drivers who have spent a lifetime chasing success in NASCAR's top series.

Ryan Newman has made an earlier, grander entrance to the sport than the two foremost open-wheeled prodigies who preceded him—Jeff Gordon and Tony Stewart. A virtuoso behind the steering wheel—like the young Mozart at the piano—Newman won the pole for the Coca-Cola 600 at Charlotte in 2001, in his third attempt to qualify for a Winston Cup race. In doing so, he tied veteran Mark Martin for the earliest pole in a career.

Competing in seven races for owner Roger Penske in 2001, Newman posted a second-place finish at Kansas City and a fifth at Michigan. Though Newman was hardly a household word in stock car racing circles, that sort of immediate success surprised no one familiar with his career in USAC cars.

Already a member of the Quarter-Midget Hall of Fame, Newman is the only USAC driver ever to win Rookie of the Year honors in the Midget, Sprint and Silver Bullet series. In 1999, he won the Coors Light Silver Bullet national championship, and, in the same year, he became the first driver to win at least one race in all three major USAC divisions: Silver Bullet, Midget and Sprint Cars.

In 2000, Newman made his stock car debut in an ARCA race in Michigan. In his second outing he won—at Pocono, Pennsylvania. Before the season was over, he collected two more victories, at Kentucky Speedway and at Lowe's Motor

| STATS (SINCE 1997) | | | | | |
|---|---|---|---|---|---|
| YEAR | STARTS | WINS | TOP 5 | TOP 10 | MONEY |
| 2001 | 7 | 0 | 2 | 2 | $466,276 |
| 2000 | 1 | 0 | 0 | 0 | $37,825 |
| 1999 | did not compete | | | | |
| 1998 | did not compete | | | | |
| 1997 | did not compete | | | | |
| TOTAL | 8 | 0 | 3 | 3 | $504,101 |

Speedway in Charlotte.

Concurrent with his introduction to Winston Cup racing in 2001, Newman also entered 15 Busch races, winning once (in the fourth race of the year at Atlanta) and claiming six pole positions.

Small wonder he consistently qualified near the head of the pack during the first five weeks of 2002.

Coincidentally, both Newman and his crew chief, Matt Borland, hold degrees in engineering. Newman got his Bachelor of Science in Vehicle Structural Engineering from Purdue University, where he graduated in August 2001.

Newman believes the formal education will play an important role in his success as a Winston Cup driver.

"Take that information and that education, and couple it with the track experience that Rusty has, and [Wallace's crew chief] Bill Wilburn—being a great racer and race car driver himself—and we've got a pretty good package of education and seat-of-the-pants experience. I think that will make us a great team for the future."

Perhaps so, but Newman's performance thus far will make it extremely difficult for him to improve on the present. The only thing currently lacking on his resume is a victory, and Newman seems certain to remedy that omission soon.

*Ryan Newman focuses on the job at hand as he waits for the green flag.*

## 12

Birthdate: December 8, 1977
Birthplace: South Bend, IN
Team: Penske Racing
Sponsor: ALLTEL
Owner: Roger Penske
Crew Chief: Matt Borland
Car: Ford

# Ricky RUDD

**If any driver in the Winston Cup garage could adopt Frank Sinatra's "My Way" as a theme song, Ricky Rudd would be the ideal candidate, now that Dave Marcis has retired.**

Though he his driven for some of the most renowned owners in stock car racing—Junie Donlavey, Richard Childress, Bud Moore, Kenny Bernstein, Rick Hendrick and Robert Yates—Rudd has essentially done it "his way" ever since he first climbed behind the steering wheel of a Winston Cup stock car in 1975.

Driving the No. 10 Ford owned by Bill Champion, the 18-year-old Rudd qualified 26th at Rockingham and parlayed that middle-of-the-pack start into an 11th-place finish, 56 laps down to race winner Cale Yarborough. Though Rudd would compete in only eight Cup races over the next two years, his performance at Rockingham was a solid indication of great things to come.

From 1976 through 1978, Rudd drove cars owned by his father, Al Rudd Sr. With ten top-ten finishes in 25 races in 1977, he claimed the Winston Cup Rookie of the Year title. Driving for Donlavey, his father, and Bill Gardner, respectively, in 1979, 1980 and 1981, Rudd failed to win a race, but he finished second three times and earned sixth place in the championship standings in Gardner's No. 88 DiGard car (a Buick, Oldsmobile or Chevrolet, depending on the race).

Rudd signed with the fledgling Childress organization in 1982, and a year later, the Chesapeake, Virginia, driver won his first race on June 5 on the 2.62-mile road course at Riverside (California) International Raceway. Appropriately, Rudd would earn the reputation throughout his career as one of the top road-course racers on the Winston Cup circuit.

Rudd won his second race later that year at Martinsville, the site of his eye-opening debut eight years earlier. His 1983 victories marked the beginning of a 16-year streak that would see Rudd win at least one race per season through 1998, his penultimate year as an owner/driver. Ironically, Rudd has never won more than two races in a single season in his 28-year career.

A remarkably consistent performer, Rudd has finished in the top ten in the championship standings 18 times. He came closest to winning the Winston Cup title in 1991, when he finished second in the No. 5 Hendrick Chevy, 195 points behind Series champion Dale Earnhardt.

Ten years later, in his second season with Yates after six years as an owner/driver, Rudd was eventual-champion Jeff Gordon's closest pursuer until mechanical problems at the Brickyard and at Michigan dimmed his title hopes.

Signing on with Yates in 2000 energized a career that had spiraled into mediocrity under the pressure of simultaneously running the team and driving the race car. From a sixth-place finish in the points in 1996, Rudd had slipped to 17th in 1997, 22nd in 1998 and 31st in 1999—almost in inverse proportion to the escalating cost of keeping a competitive race team on the track.

Though he failed to win a race in his first season behind the wheel of Yates' powerful No. 28 Ford, Rudd improved to fifth in the championship standings. In his battle with Gordon in 2001, he returned to Victory Lane for the first time in 88 races—at Martinsville, no less—and followed that with a win at Richmond, where he played bumper tag with rookie Kevin Harvick, whom he passed for the lead with six laps remaining.

**28**

Birthdate: September 12, 1956

Birthplace: Chesapeake, VA

Team: Robert Yates Racing

Sponsor: Havoline

Owner: Robert Yates

Crew Chief: Michael McSwain

Car: Ford

*Ricky Rudd shed the pressure of competing as an owner/driver when he took over the controls of Robert Yates' No. 28 Ford.*

## Ricky **RUDD**

Rudd began the 2002 campaign recuperating from back surgery to repair a bulging disc in his lower back. Rudd had woken up one morning during race week at Dover, Delaware, and noticed a pain he had never experienced before.

"I just figured I must have slept on it wrong," says

# I thought, 'I'll get through today and get a good night's sleep, and it will get better.' Well, it never got better.

Rudd, who celebrated his 45th birthday in September 2001. "I thought, 'I'll get through today and get a good night's sleep, and it will get better.' Well, it never got better. It went on for over six months. It never really got worse, but it never got better.

"Kind of an odd thing, something I wasn't used to dealing with. It's hell to get old. I guess that's what it is."

With Yates power under his hood, however, and one of the strongest organizations in the garage, Rudd undoubtedly has more than a few good years left.

**Ricky Rudd's Ford is little more than a blur as it flashes past the grandstand.**

## STATS (SINCE 1997)

| YEAR | STARTS | WINS | TOP 5 | TOP 10 | MONEY |
|------|--------|------|-------|--------|-------|
| 2001 | 36 | 2 | 14 | 22 | $4,878,027 |
| 2000 | 34 | 0 | 12 | 19 | $2,974,970 |
| 1999 | 34 | 0 | 3 | 5 | $1,632,011 |
| 1998 | 33 | 1 | 1 | 5 | $1,602,895 |
| 1997 | 32 | 2 | 6 | 11 | $1,975,981 |
| CAREER | 731 | 22 | 179 | 344 | $24,590,223 |

# Elliott SADLER

**As long as Elliott Sadler has been racing, it is difficult to believe he just turned 27 in April 2002.**

The younger brother of veteran Busch Series driver Hermie Sadler, the Emporia, Virginia, native began his career in go-karts at age seven and won more than 200 races before trying his hand in a stock car in 1993. South Boston (Va.) Speedway has proved a fertile training ground over the years, and Sadler was yet another beneficiary of the intense weekend competition there.

In 1995, he won 13 races and the track championship in late model stocks. He also got his first taste of competition in the Busch Series that year, when NASCAR's second-tier road show visited South Boston. By 1997, Sadler was a full-time competitor in the Busch Series, and he made the most of his opportunity—winning three races and finishing fifth in the championship standings.

The 1998 season brought two more Busch Series victories and his debut in the Winston Cup. Driving a car owned by Gary Bechtel, Sadler qualified 31st for the May 24 Coca-Cola 600 at Charlotte and finished 42nd in his first appearance in NASCAR's top series. At the end of the season, Sadler began a long-term association with the vaunted Wood Brothers team when he competed in the Coca-Cola 200 exhibition race on the road course at Motegi, Japan; he started fourth and finished 20th.

Running a full schedule with the Wood Brothers in 1999, Sadler posted one top-ten and finished second to Tony Stewart in the battle for Rookie of the Year honors. But the promise of 1999 dissolved into disappointment in 2000, when Sadler failed to qualify for the first race at Talladega and failed to finish four other races. With one top-ten to his credit in 33 races, Sadler was 29th in points—and highly motivated to improve in 2001.

True enough, the 2001 season produced several milestones for Sadler and his team. After wrecking his primary car and starting 38th in a provisional, he posted his first Winston Cup victory in his 75th start, at Bristol on March 25. That was the Wood Brothers' first trip to Victory Lane since Morgan Shepherd won at Atlanta on March 20, 1993.

Sadler finished a career-best 20th in points in 2001 and matched his best-ever qualifying effort on back-to-back weekends at Michigan and Bristol, where he started fourth. When Dale Earnhardt Jr. took the checkered flag at the end of the emotionally-charged Pepsi 400 at Daytona in July, Sadler crossed the finish line third.

The victory at Bristol, coupled with a year's experience with crew chief Pat Tryson, gave Sadler a healthy dose of confidence entering the 2002 season.

"I've got a lot more confidence going into this year than I did last year," Sadler said. "Last year we didn't know what to expect. We had never had a win. It was the first year that Pat and I had worked together. This year we're all on the same page—everybody on the team.

"We really feel that we've got our stuff in a line. We've got the right cars lined up for the right racetracks. That's good. We needed that. So I feel a lot better right now than I did a year ago."

**In his fourth season in Winston Cup racing, Elliott Sadler scored his first career victory at Bristol.**

## STATS (SINCE 1997)

| YEAR | STARTS | WINS | TOP 5 | TOP 10 | MONEY |
|------|--------|------|-------|--------|-------|
| 2001 | 36 | 1 | 2 | 2 | $2,683,225 |
| 2000 | 33 | 0 | 0 | 1 | $1,578,356 |
| 1999 | 34 | 0 | 0 | 1 | $1,589,221 |
| 1998 | 2 | 0 | 0 | 0 | $45,325 |
| 1997 | did not compete | | | | |
| **CAREER** | **105** | **1** | **2** | **4** | **$5,896,127** |

Birthdate: April 30, 1975

Birthplace: Emporia, VA

Team: Wood Brothers Racing

Sponsor: Motorcraft

Owners: Glen Wood, Eddie Wood, Len Wood, Kim Wood Hall

Crew Chief: Pat Tryson

Car: Ford

# Jimmy SPENCER

**Forget that Jimmy Spencer, a.k.a. "Mr Excitement," hasn't been to the winner's circle since 1994. In the eyes of his peers, he's one of the most respected competitors in the Winston Cup garage.**

When the late Dale Earnhardt used to indulge in "recreational" racing in the dirt on his North Carolina farm, Spencer was a frequent participant. But more often than not, there has been a "restrictor plate" on Spencer's career; the equipment he drives seldom lives up to his talent.

A two-time NASCAR Winston Modified Series champion (1986 and 1987), Spencer spent the early days of his Winston Cup career driving for under-funded operations. After a full-time stint in the Busch Series in 1988, he got his Winston Cup start in 1989, posting three top-tens in 17 races for owner Buddy Baker; but lack of sponsorship eventually put Spencer on the sidelines.

He entered 24 races in 1990 in Rod Osterlund's No. 57 Pontiac, with a pair of top-ten results. The following season brought his first association with owner Travis Carter, for whom Spencer would later drive for seven straight years. In 29 races with Carter, Spencer notched his first career top-five—at North Wilkesboro, where he drove Carter's No. 98 Chevrolet to a third-place finish.

After seven races for Carter and one for Dick Moroso in 1992, Spencer's career received a boost when he climbed behind the wheel of Bobby Allison's No. 12 Ford with four races left on the schedule. Given the opportunity to showcase his talent, Spencer promptly finished fourth at Charlotte, 11th at Rockingham, fifth at Phoenix and fourth at Atlanta. When the Winston Cup circuit opened the 1993 season at Daytona, Spencer was Allison's full-time driver.

## STATS (SINCE 1997)

| YEAR | STARTS | WINS | TOP 5 | TOP 10 | MONEY |
|---|---|---|---|---|---|
| 2001 | 36 | 0 | 3 | 8 | $2,669,638 |
| 2000 | 34 | 0 | 2 | 5 | $1,936,762 |
| 1999 | 34 | 0 | 2 | 4 | $1,752,299 |
| 1998 | 31 | 0 | 3 | 8 | $1,741,012 |
| 1997 | 32 | 0 | 1 | 4 | $1,073,779 |
| **CAREER** | **370** | **2** | **25** | **70** | **$12,747,382** |

With a second-place result at Talladega, thirds at Watkins Glen and Martinsville, a pair of fourths at Bristol and Pocono, and five other top-tens, Spencer finished the season a career-best 12th in the championship standings.

Spencer drove for Junior Johnson in 1994, and that association brought the only two victories of his career, both at restrictor-plate tracks. In the Pepsi 400 at Daytona, he edged Ernie Irvan in a furious battle to the finish line. At Talladega he beat Bill Elliott to the checkered flag.

The 1995 season brought a reunion with Carter and the start of a seven-year drought. Spencer finished second twice during that span, but could do no better than 14th in points (1998).

"We never clicked to the point of winning," Spencer says. It came as no surprise when Mr Excitement jumped at the chance to drive for Chip Ganassi in 2002—on the recommendation of his friend Sterling Marlin.

"When Felix [Sabates] started asking him … he said, 'I like old Spence,'" Spencer explained. "… I still have the desire to drive the wheels off [the car]. The day is going to come when I'm going to say to myself, 'I'm just tired of this and I don't like it any more'—but I think that's a long time away."

**Jimmy Spencer earned the nickname "Mr. Excitement" for his aggressive driving style.**

## 41

Birthdate: February 15, 1957
Birthplace: Berwick, PA
Team: Chip Ganassi Racing
Sponsor: Target
Owners: Chip Ganassi, Felix Sabates
Crew Chief: Doug Randolph
Car: Dodge

# Tony STEWART

**When tempestuous Tony Stewart arrived on the Winston Cup scene with all the fanfare that usually accompanies a coronation, he arrived with an abundance of self-confidence—and a petulant attitude to go with it.**

**B**ut his no-holds-barred talk and occasional explosions of temper quickly took a back seat to one of the most remarkable rookie seasons in Winston Cup history. It's not enough to note that Stewart won the Rookie of the Year title in a landslide. For one thing, with victories at Richmond, Phoenix and Homestead in a stunning second half of the 1999 season, the Rushville (Indiana) Rocket became the first ever driver to win three races during his rookie campaign.

With an astounding 13 top-five finishes and 21 top-tens, he finished fourth in the final points standings, proving that he had made the difficult transition from open-wheeled cars to stock cars without missing a beat.

Stewart's racing resume dates to 1983, when, at age 12, he won the International Karting Foundation Grand National championship. His progress through the ranks was meteoric. In 1993, he won his first USAC Midget feature in Terre Haute, Indiana. By the time the 1995 season ended, he was national champion in USAC's Midget, Sprint and Silver Crown series; no driver before him had ever won the title in all three divisions in the same season.

In 1996, Stewart was Rookie of the Year for the Indianapolis 500, where he won the pole and led the first 44 laps. In 1997, he was Indy Racing League champion.

As Stewart prepared for his eventual move to Winston Cup racing, he split his time between the Busch Series and the Indy Racing League. Though he was a full-time Winston Cup driver in 1999, he nevertheless ran the Indianapolis 500 and NASCAR's Coca-Cola 600 on the same day (May 30),

completing 1,090 of a possible 1,100 miles in the two races. After finishing ninth at Indy, Stewart jetted to Charlotte, where he battled to a fourth-place finish.

The 2000 season brought a series-best six victories—at both Dover races, Michigan, New Hampshire, Martinsville and Homestead—and solidified Stewart's reputation as perhaps the best "flat-track" driver in the Winston Cup Series. Despite his prolific number of victories, however, Stewart slipped to sixth in points, a result that can be directly attributed to his failure to finish five races.

A late-season surge in 2001 gave Stewart his best points finish to date, second to champion Jeff Gordon. Stewart added three more victories to his growing list of accomplishments—on the road course at Sears Point (Sonoma, California), at Richmond and at Bristol. Astoundingly, he actually improved on his 1999 "daily double" at Indianapolis and Charlotte when he finished sixth in the Indy 500 and third in the Coca-Cola 600, completing all 1,100 miles.

As the 2002 season approached, the brash 30 year old with a penchant for bowling, cheeseburgers and video games made a conscious effort to present a kinder, gentler image—thanks perhaps to the influence of car owner Joe Gibbs, the former Washington Redskins coach whose strait-laced demeanor has provided a sharp contrast to his impetuous driver's lack of restraint.

Stewart is also quick to point out that the interaction between Gibbs' two teams has much to do with the success of both enterprises. The organization includes 2000 Winston Cup champion Bobby Labonte (with long-time crew chief Jimmy Makar) and Stewart (with one of the most effective young crew chiefs in the garage, Greg Zipadelli).

"When Joe started the two-car team and put them under one roof and showed how Jimmy and Bobby and Greg and I, how we all four mingled and talked to each other—I think

## 20

Birthdate: May 20, 1971
Birthplace: Columbus, IN
Team: Joe Gibbs Racing
Sponsor: Home Depot
Owner: Joe Gibbs
Crew Chief: Greg Zipadelli
Car: Pontiac

**Everything about Tony Stewart is explosive—from his talent to his temperament.**

it showed how multi-car teams are the way of the future for our sport," Stewart says.

Stewart also announced his intention to try to eliminate outside distractions during the 2002 season, the implication being that if a reporter doesn't shove a tape recorder under his nose as soon as he climbs out of his car, Stewart won't grab the offending machine and throw it beneath a nearby transporter (as he once did).

> **Being volatile doesn't make you a good race driver. Winning races makes you a good race car driver.**

"If it doesn't make the race car go faster or doesn't promote Home Depot (his sponsor), I'm not doing it," he said. I'm not messing with the outside distractions…"

"Being volatile doesn't make you a good race driver. Winning races makes you a good race car driver. The distractions outside the car are what make me volatile, so we're eliminating the distractions."

Don't bet on even-tempered Tony to stay that way. Then again, don't bet against a championship for the versatile phenom.

**Tony Stewart visited Victory Lane three times in his rookie year.**

## STATS (SINCE 1997)

| YEAR | STARTS | WINS | TOP 5 | TOP 10 | MONEY |
|------|--------|------|-------|--------|-------|
| 2001 | 36 | 3 | 15 | 22 | $4,941,463 |
| 2000 | 34 | 6 | 12 | 23 | $3,642,348 |
| 1999 | 34 | 3 | 12 | 21 | $3,190,149 |
| 1998 | did not compete | | | | |
| 1997 | did not compete | | | | |
| CAREER | 104 | 12 | 39 | 66 | $11,773,960 |

# Rusty WALLACE

**In Winston Cup racing, "50" is the magic number. It's the passkey to the elite inner circle of stock car racing legends, a one-way ticket to the Hall of Fame.**

Drivers with 50 or more career victories occupy a special place in Winston Cup lore, because so few among the hundreds who have attempted to win even one race have reached the lofty number of 50.

In more than 50 years of NASCAR racing, only 11 men have won 50 or more times. Of the active drivers on the Winston Cup circuit, only two have reached that milestone. One is four-time Winston Cup champion Jeff Gordon, who stood seventh on the all-time list with 58 victories through 2001.

The other is veteran Rusty Wallace, the garrulous short-track specialist who, at the pinnacle of his proficiency, won ten races in 1993. Through the 2001 season, Wallace had 54 victories to his credit—ninth on the career list and immediately ahead of such luminaries as Ned Jarrett and Junior Johnson, who posted 50 wins each.

The son of a racing father, Wallace learned his craft at Lakehill Speedway in Valley Park, Missouri, where he won more than 200 stock car features between 1974 and 1978. In 1979 he joined the USAC stock car series and claimed the Rookie of the Year title with five victories.

In 1980, Wallace made his debut in the Winston Cup in a car owned by Roger Penske. He finished second to 1980 Series champion Dale Earnhardt on March 16 at Atlanta. Wallace also raced for Penske in the National 500 at Charlotte that year, starting 15th and finishing 14th. Eleven years would pass before Wallace would race for Penske in the Winston Cup Series again.

After winning the American Speed Association champi-onship in 1983, Wallace made his formal graduation to Winston Cup in 1984, driving a full schedule in Cliff Stewart's No. 88 Pontiac. After a second winless season in 1985, Wallace accepted a ride from owner Raymond Beadle in the No. 27 Blue Max Racing Pontiac.

It was on April 6, 1986 that Wallace recorded his first career victory at Bristol and began to establish his reputation as a master of the short tracks. He won again on September 21 at Martinsville.

From 1986 on, Wallace has won at least one event per year. In 1988, still driving for Beadle, he finished second to Bill Elliott in one of the closest championship races in Winston Cup history—Wallace ended the season 24 points behind Awesome Bill.

In 1989, Wallace edged Dale Earnhardt for his only Series title by an even closer margin—12 points. In winning six races during his championship run, Wallace became only the eighth driver in Winston Cup history to exceed $5 million in prize money—a total that today represents a single-season total for a top driver.

The championship battle came down to the season's final race at Atlanta, where Wallace had to finish no more than 18 places behind Earnhardt to clinch the title. Earnhardt won the race itself—an event clouded by the death of driver Grant Adcox after a fiery crash on lap 202—but Wallace rallied to finish 15th and secured the championship.

Wallace parted with Beadle after a sixth-place finish in points in 1990 and began an association with Penske that has lasted more than a decade. He was second in points in 1993, 80 behind Earnhardt, despite his ten victories. In 1994, Wallace added eight more wins to his side of the ledger. After winning two events in 1995 and five in 1996, Wallace posted one victory per year in 1997, 1998 and 1999 before returning to form and winning four times in 2000.

**2**

Birthdate: August 19, 1956

Birthplace: St. Louis, MO

Team: Penske Racing

Sponsor: Miller Lite

Owner: Roger Penske

Crew Chief: Bill Wilburn

Car: Ford

**Rusty Wallace is one of two active drivers to have reached the 50-win milestone.**

## Rusty **Wallace**

Lean times returned in 2001, the same year Wallace reached his 45th birthday, though he won his only race of the year at California Speedway, a track built by, and owned by, Penske.

Missing from Wallace's list of accomplishments is a victory at either of the restrictor-plate superspeedways—Daytona or Talladega—though Wallace has provided his share of highlights at each of the facilities.

His spectacular barrel rolls past the start/finish line at Talladega in May 1993 helped to speed up the introduction of a new safety feature mandated by NASCAR—roof flaps

# I've won just about everywhere except Daytona

designed to prevent cars from becoming airborne in a high-speed crash.

Though Wallace has a championship to his credit, he believes a victory in the Daytona 500 would be a capstone to his career.

"Yes, absolutely, I think so," Wallace says. "I've won just about everywhere except Daytona and should have won Daytona three or four times but didn't do it... We've got good horsepower, good cars, fast pit crews, the whole thing—all the resources we need to get the job done. We've just got to get all the moons lined up in the right angle to win this thing."

**The Miller Lite Ford is always a threat to win.**

### STATS (SINCE 1997)

| YEAR | STARTS | WINS | TOP 5 | TOP 10 | MONEY |
|---|---|---|---|---|---|
| 2001 | 36 | 1 | 8 | 14 | $4,788,652 |
| 2000 | 34 | 4 | 12 | 20 | $3,621,468 |
| 1999 | 34 | 1 | 7 | 16 | $2,454,050 |
| 1998 | 33 | 1 | 15 | 21 | $2,667,889 |
| 1997 | 32 | 1 | 8 | 12 | $1,705,625 |
| CAREER | 562 | 54 | 182 | 292 | $29,657,719 |

# Michael WALTRIP

**If 50 victories make up the measure of greatness for a Winston Cup driver, what is the measure of mediocrity?**

For Michael Waltrip, that number was 462—the number of points races he had started without a victory in his Winston Cup career.

But that was before the season-opening Daytona 500 of 2001, where Waltrip's thrill of victory played out against a backdrop of tragedy.

As Waltrip and Dale Earnhardt Jr. sped toward the checkered flag, Dale Earnhardt Sr., running behind the two leaders, collided with Sterling Marlin and Ken Schrader and hit the wall in the final turn.

As Waltrip crossed the finish line to win his first race in his 463rd start—while brother Darrell Waltrip called the action from the broadcast booth—the elder Earnhardt, owner of the cars driven by his son and by Waltrip, sat lifeless in his legendary No. 3 Chevrolet.

Inspired by the confidence Earnhardt had shown in him, Waltrip won the most prestigious prize in stock car racing. And now Earnhardt was gone.

Almost as a memorial to the fallen hero, a similar scenario unfolded in the Pepsi 400 at Daytona in July 2001. This time it was Earnhardt Jr. who took the checkered flag, with team-mate Waltrip shepherding him to the finish line in second place.

"That's the way it was supposed to be done, right there," Waltrip said after the race. "Dale Earnhardt laid back there in third place and fought the battle of his life at the Daytona 500 for me and Dale Jr. to get home.

"And I was having to fight my rear end off. But the NAPA Chevy pushed Dale Jr. home and that's what we were hoping for. I knew my car was good, but you never know if

| STATS (SINCE 1997) | | | | | |
|---|---|---|---|---|---|
| **YEAR** | **STARTS** | **WINS** | **TOP 5** | **TOP 10** | **MONEY** |
| 2001 | 36 | 1 | 3 | 3 | $3,411,644 |
| 2000 | 34 | 0 | 1 | 1 | $1,689,421 |
| 1999 | 34 | 0 | 1 | 3 | $1,701,160 |
| 1998 | 32 | 0 | 0 | 5 | $1,508,680 |
| 1997 | 32 | 0 | 0 | 6 | $1,138,599 |
| **CAREER** | **498** | **1** | **21** | **85** | **$14,827,176** |

you're going to get a hole. You could get locked in. You never know. I just did my part, man, and the team did theirs."

Clearly, the bittersweet 2001 campaign was Waltrip's most successful. Driving for most of his career in the shadow of his brother Darrell, who won 84 races and three championships before retiring to the broadcast booth, Waltrip in 2001 added a second-place finish at Homestead to his list of accomplishments.

Collectively, those were his best results since a second-place finish at Pocono in 1988 in Chuck Rider's No. 30 Bahari Racing Pontiac. Waltrip has never finished above 12th in the championship standings, a high watermark he attained in consecutive years with Bahari in 1994 and 1995.

Before his Daytona 500 victory, Waltrip would have to consider his 1996 win in The Winston at Charlotte (a non-points race) his foremost accomplishment in Winston Cup. Waltrip became the first ever driver to win The Winston after transferring from the Winston Open. He also won $1 million in a single season for the first time in 1996.

On balance, though, it has been a long and often frustrating career for the affable driver from Kentucky, who claimed his first significant title in 1983 when he won the NASCAR Goody's Dash Series championship.

But the inspiration of Dale Earnhardt lives within Waltrip, and with it lives the promise of better days to come.

**Michael Waltrip notched his first victory at the 2001 Daytona 500, in his 463rd career start.**

15

Birthdate: April 30, 1963
Birthplace: Owensboro, KY
Team: Dale Earnhardt Incorporated
Sponsor: NAPA Auto Parts
Owner: Teresa Earnhardt
Crew Chief: Slugger Labbe
Car: Chevrolet

**PICTURE CREDITS**

The publishers would like to thank the following sources for their kind permission to reproduce the pictures in this book.

**Getty Images**: 6, 16, 19, 20, 21, 22, 23, 24, 27, 27b, 28, 29, 31, 33, 41, 42, 45, 57, 61, 63, 65, 67, 69, 71, 73, 75, 79, 81, 83, 85, 87, 89.

**Sutton Motorsports**: 4, 14, 15, 35, 36, 37, 39, 41, 46, 47, 48, 49, 50, 51, 52, 55, 59, 69, 75b, 77, 91, 93, 95, 96

**Dozier Mobley Archive**: 8, 10, 11, 12